Team Pupil in School

THE ATTACHMENT AWARE SCHOOL SERIES
Bridging the gap for troubled pupils

Book 1 The Key Adult in School
Book 2 The Senior Manager in School
Book 3 The Key Teacher in School
Book 4 Team Pupil in School
Book 5 The Parent and Carer in School

**Other books in the
Attachment Aware Schools Collection®**

ATTACHMENT AWARE SCHOOLS COLLECTION®

Attachment in the Classroom
Better Play
Conversations That Matter
Inside I'm Hurting
Little-Mouse Finds a Safe Place
School as a Secure Base
Settling to Learn
Teaching the Unteachable
Teenagers and Attachment
Temper Temper!
What About Me?
What Can I Do With The Kid Who…?
You think I'm Evil

ATTACHMENT AWARE SCHOOL SERIES
Bridging the gap for troubled pupils

Book 4

Team Pupil in School

Louise Michelle Bombèr

First published 2016 by Worth Publishing Ltd
worthpublishing.com

© Worth Publishing Ltd 2016

All rights reserved. No part of this publication may be reproduced, stored in a retrieval system or transmitted in any form, or by any means, electronic, mechanical, photocopying, recording or otherwise, without the prior permission of the publishers, nor be otherwise circulated without the publisher's consent in any form of binding or cover other than that in which it is published and without a similar condition being imposed on the subsequent purchaser.

Printed and bound in Great Britain by TJ International,
Padstow, Cornwall

British Library Cataloguing in Publication Data
A catalogue record for this book is available from the British Library
ISBN   9781903269312

Cover and text design by Anna Murphy

For Jane Airey,
who played a significant role
in my journey

Biography

Louise Michelle Bombèr is a specialist Attachment Lead Teacher and a therapist. She has worked for many years with children and young people who have experienced significant relational traumas and losses. Working in many different contexts she is passionate about ensuring these pupils have opportunity to adapt and recover so that they can make the most of all that school offers. She continues to work as a practitioner using Theraplay®, PACE, DDP and sensory interventions to support children and their parents.

Louise is the author of *Inside I'm Hurting*, *What About Me?*, co-author with Dr Dan Hughes of *Settling to Learn* and contributor to *Teenagers and Attachment*. Her work has been greatly influenced by John Bowlby, Dan Hughes, Daniel Siegel, Bruce Perry and Gabor Maté. Louise advises, trains and supports education professionals and families, and is involved in direct work with children and young people in class, in the therapy room and at an allotment project, PLOT 22 (*and see* touchbase.org.uk). She heads up a network which enables Attachment Leads to be trained to provide advocacy and support in individual schools across the UK (attachmentleadnetwork.net).

Acknowledgements

Thanks to Dr Kim Golding for her continued partnership with me, and my long standing supervisor Penny Auton, who has walked alongside me in my professional journey over many, many years. I would like to thank Jenny Peters in the UK and Glen Cooper in the USA for generously providing me with commentary on Circle of Security®, which is such an invaluable resource to all those wanting to make a difference in children's lives.

I would like to honour all those parents and carers that have shared their stories so vulnerably with me over the years as to what it is like to parent these children. I admire you and so wish that your children could see what I see, how much you deeply love them and root for them and how you desire for them to know how much they are valued, special and that they 'belong' to your family. This is so hard for them to take in.

My current TouchBase™ team - Jennie Fellows, Julia Wilde, Keeley de Freese, Becs Uvieghara, Natalie Miller, Tania Druce,

Alice Mallorie and Henrietta Kuhudzai for your dedication and commitment to these children; it doesn't go unnoticed. My national trainers, Anne Henderson, Clare Langhorne, Alison Lumley, Helen Wallace and Helen Wright who so passionately deliver materials they believe in, whilst continuing as practitioners actively involved with many pupils. All the support assistants and mentors with whom I have journeyed since 2000; together we have learned what is needed.

My editor and friend Andrea Perry who encourages and mobilises me into further creativity. My husband Jonathan Fordham, who often releases me from household responsibilities because he believes in this cause as much as I do. Thanks for holding the fort when I bury my head in books and my laptop! Lucinda and Steve Smith who lead with both gentleness and strength, continuing to be really behind my vision to see dignity restored. Nothing goes unnoticed.

All the brave families who have endured more than many will ever know and yet remain standing clothed in dignity and strength and armed with fierce compassion for their hurting children. May this series of books play some part in raising much needed awareness so that you can take a step back, trusting the schools your children attend to nurture them into all they should have been first time around.

Foreword

Team Pupil in School is the fourth book in the **Attachment Aware School Series**. Here Louise brings together the team described individually in the previous books. She provides clear direction for how to help these individual professionals work together to help their Key Pupil. In doing so, she also provides advice on how they can support each other. They need to work well together within a system that does not always appreciate their endeavours. This is a book that is realistic, as well as aspirational.

Children with relational traumas have the hardest times in our schools. They go to school to learn, but they can only achieve their learning potential through the relationships that they have. Just pause for a moment and reflect on this. These are the children who have been hurt by the relationships that were meant to cherish, protect and nurture them. These children are strong and resilient. They learnt to survive and they bring this learning into school. This is survival, however, disconnected from other people. This is survival, without the realisation of full potential. Education is at its best when it is relational. Children need support in school. Children with relational traumas will resist these relationships. This is the challenge that faces **Team Pupil**.

Individuals within **Team Pupil** will take on this challenge. They will persist in their offer of relationship to the pupils, even though the pupils will initially reject their offer; rejection which can come in the most challenging of ways. Individual members of the **Team** will only be able to continue to offer this support if they have relationships to strengthen them. The **Team** around the pupil will provide relational support to each other whilst helping the pupils to risk some relationship experience themselves. Only then can education begin.

For me **Team Pupil** is about the unsung heroes. We see the pupils, the challenges that they present, the achievements that they make. Behind these pupils sit these **Teams**. At the time of writing, the Rio Olympics are just drawing to a close. I have been privileged to watch the most talented of athletes achieve the pinnacle of their dreams. Behind each of these athletes sits a team of people without whom these achievements would not happen. The athletes shine, whilst the team around them quietly support. Like the athletes, the pupil's success will be measured in their achievements. These achievements will not come without the relational support **Team Pupil** can offer; support that over time can help their pupils to shine.

All unsung heroes need support of their own, and this is what Louise can offer. Support to understand; support to believe; and ultimately, support to achieve. **Team Pupil** and its place in the **Attachment Aware School Series** provides timely, clear and practical support which will help the team work together; to continue to offer what the pupils need, even in the darkest hours. Success is hard won, but with the **Team** working together, supported by Louise's advice and guidance, I truly believe that more relationally traumatised children can stand on their own personal podiums. They can achieve all that they are capable of during their time in school.

Kim S. Golding, August 2016

Team Pupil in school

Please note: In this book I reference material from my earlier publications, using acronyms for their titles for accessibility. These books form a key resource for developing attachment awareness and trauma informed interventions in schools, and provide background reading for the **Attachment Aware School Series.**

Inside I'm Hurting	(2007)	(**IIH**)
What About Me?	(2011)	(**WAM**)
Settling to Learn (*with* Dan Hughes)	(2013)	(**STL**)
Key Adult in School	(2015)	(**KAiS**)
Key Teacher in School	(2016)	(**KT**)
Senior Manager in School	(2016)	(**SM**)
Parent and Carer in School	(2016)	(**PC**)
Teenagers & Attachment (*in* Perry, Ed.)	(2009)	(**TA**)

Contents

Introduction		1
PART 1	**Becoming an effective Team Pupil**	19
	Core aims of **Team Pupil**	21
	Ideal qualities of **Team Pupil** members	22
	Good questions about how **Team Pupil** works in practice	23
PART 2	**The attachment aware, trauma informed Team Pupil in practice**	31
	Responsibilities of **Team Pupil**	32
	10 things others say about the work of **Team Pupil**	58

continues/...

PART 3	**Facilitating the best outcomes**	**59**
	A Holding boundaries	62
	EXERCISE to build self-awareness	63
	B Working in a partnership to settle the pupil	65
	C Resilience	70
	D Advocacy	75
	E Holding onto success	77

Glossary	81
References	89
Useful documents	94
Useful contacts	95

Introduction

This pocket-sized book is part of the **Attachment Aware School Series**. The series has come about in response to an increasing understanding that security, through the experience of safe and attuned relationships, is necessary for every pupil to be able to settle to learn and make the most of all the educational opportunities out there. It is only when a pupil's **attachment system** is attended to that their **exploratory system** can really come into play.

Some children may have learned security outside school through their experience of relationships to date - others may not. Some pupils find settling into learning incredibly difficult, especially those who have a history of not being attended to, or responded to sufficiently, or often enough; of neglect, traumatic experience or significant loss. If circumstances have ruptured or inhibited the development of an internal, felt sense of security, then children often experience huge anxiety - sometimes unnoted by those of

Team Pupil in school

us observing. These pupils are not in a position to learn or take up the huge range of opportunities available to them in school YET. So in school, we must first address their need for security and stability - by providing them with a consistent, reliable, empathic, attuned attachment relationship in school. Only then can we expect them to make progress with learning, and to fully engage with school life.

On really difficult days, even the most securely attached child - or adult - may find learning a struggle. So this series of pocket books endorses the view that if a school is fully attachment aware, and indeed, trauma informed (*see later*), *all pupils and staff will benefit*. Ideally all staff will have attachment aware training as their foundation, and with this background will appreciate that for some pupils a specific, targeted relational intervention will be a life-line.

In the **Attachment Aware School Series** we advocate having a small tight team around these specific pupils - **Team Pupil.** So, in school we will have Team Lee, Team Grace, Team Aiden … four or five people in different positions of responsibility in the school, all believing *in* and rooting *for* their Key Pupil.

> Having several good attachment relationships predicts better self-control, behaviour and relationships.
>
> Belsky et al 2007

In the primary phase, **Team Pupil** will usually be made up of the Key Adult, a back-up adult if appropriate, the class teacher, and a Senior Manager. In the secondary phase, this would usually be the Key Adult, the form tutor, a subject teacher and one or two Senior Managers (*and see below on choosing people for the Team,* p.9). In addition to this school-based team, each Key Pupil needs to know that their parents and carers are on board with their education, trusting those involved to support their child and actively working in tight partnership within their unique **Team**.

With this in mind, there are five books in the **Attachment Aware School Series**, each reflecting the different roles of the different individuals in the team around the Key Pupil (one for each member of the **Team**, and this book for the **Team** as a whole). The **Series** aims to help this valuable community work well together, holding the pupil in mind, shoring him or her up when necessary, serving as an anchor, so that anxieties can be relieved; freeing up the possibility for this child or young person to become all they were intended to become, first time around. I have also included a pocket book for the parents or carers of the pupil, since they will be and often are such valuable contributors to the school team.

Throughout each book you'll find some key terms are highlighted in bold; you'll find all of these in the **Glossary** on p.81.

Team Pupil in school

This particular book is intended for those who have come together to work as **Team Pupil**, and for others (for example parents and carers of children or young people who have experienced **relational trauma** and loss, and Heads who might be considering this kind of work for a pupil or pupils in their school), to learn more about what the collective **Team Pupil** approach looks like.

We now understand that both emotional growth and wellbeing are directly linked to learning. We also know that the more a child or young person experiences quality connections with mature adults, the more mature his brain becomes. Education from 5-16 is compulsory in the UK, and so these children and young people will be with us for many weeks, terms and years. So it is our professional responsibility to invest time and resources into facilitating relationally rich contexts for this particular group of pupils with challenging histories of **relational trauma** and loss.

We know now that a history of **relational trauma** and loss needn't be a life sentence of insecure attachments, developmental vulnerabilities, low educational outcomes and a compromised future. Children and young people can learn security and can negotiate and consolidate the necessary developmental milestones. But they need us alongside them to do so.

We also know from neuroscience that the richer relational experiences these pupils have, the more complex the neural pathways and connections in their brains will be, meaning that relationships bring integration. Integration brings health - physical, mental and emotional health. And richer relational experiences and more complex systems in the brain mean the pupil will be able to engage in more complex thinking, relating and being. This is the way ahead for all of us who take our pupils' wellbeing and development seriously.

> Let's shift from a behavioural view of pupils to a relational one - focusing on trying to understand what their behaviour means [or communicates].
> Hughes & Baylin 2012, p.8 (*my parantheses*)

Identifying pupils who would benefit from the Team Pupil approach

It is important that we recognise pupils who may need this type of support. Not always easy, as many have gone 'into hiding' or 'underground', lying dormant, but still troubled. Some pupils don't always present with significant difficulties, whereas others clearly do. The specific targeted support documented in these pocket books is intended for those who have experienced **relational trauma** and loss.

To understand what this means, to know who to look out for, it is probably important we distinguish between *single trauma*

Team Pupil in school

incidents and ***relational trauma*** *and loss.* Single trauma incidents could include one-off events such as being in a car crash, witnessing violence on the streets, being raped, being trapped in a burning building. These would all likely be identified as trauma. A definition of trauma that I find helpful is when someone experiences, '*intense fear, helplessness or terror*' (American Psychological Association). Powerlessness is part of the essence of trauma. But this type of trauma, though horrific and leaving the person powerless, doesn't necessarily mean **relational trauma**.

What I mean by **relational trauma** is when neglect or something else has happened repeatedly over a period of time at the hands of those close to you: for example, being sexually abused by your dad, being beaten up by your mum, being scorned and humiliated by your step-mum. These types of traumas leave the person even more powerless and vulnerable, since at times of distress, our attachment response is activated, pushing us to seek proximity with those closest to us for safety, reassurance and support. So what does a child or young person do if their **attachment figure** is actually his or her abuser? When the child uses proximity-seeking behaviours but is ignored? How desperately confusing and terrifying this must be. Where can the child or young person go then? He or she will become more and more isolated, with no possibility or opportunity for the trauma to be resolved. The child or young person may learn they need to rely on themselves; they may develop a false, pseudo-independence, because it is not safe to seek proximity with those closest to them, or to depend on them.

Those who have experienced this type of trauma enter a state of what some call *complicated grieving*. They find it hard to trust adults, especially those unsuspecting people who may take on a care-giving, nurturing role, even when the abuser has been taken out of the equation: for example foster carers, adoptive parents, support staff …

These children expect adults to actively hurt them, to leave them in distress, to make them feel worse and to even terrorise them: because this has been their experience, in the closest of relationships, where they should have been able to expect support. The closer an adult gets to them, the more they will expect hurt and distress to happen. As I mentioned earlier, this expectation won't always be explicitly presented in their behaviour. Human beings are complex and find numerous survival strategies to defend against vulnerability. So we have children out there who are very compliant, helping at every opportunity. We have children out there who need to please, complimenting you frequently, or making you smile or laugh. Don't be fooled! Some of these children are doing all they can to keep you sweet, in case you find them too much, or you may turn on them or walk away. Their defences are fuelled by high levels of anxiety.

Team Pupil in school

These particular children have been wounded in the context of relationship to those closest to them. They will therefore need close relationships and many significant, rich relational experiences now to *disconfirm* everything they have learned previously. Hence the need for a Key Adult in school, to give the pupil the opportunity to build a close relationship with him or her. Some children and young people will need a back-up adult too, if some of their behaviour is challenging and disruptive, to allow for swap-ins.

Having been advocating for and supporting the development of Key Adult relationships for a long time now, over the last few years I have observed how powerful it can be if these children and young people *also* receive wraparound, consistent care from a handful of others, in addition to the Key Adult. It is easy for these pupils to get 'lost' in the big system of school if they only have their Key Adult, and everyone else has a hands-off approach. These pupils need a small family system created for them, **Team Pupil**, whereby each member has their own unique role and responsibilities in regard to the Key Pupil, just like a usual healthy family might.

Please use the flowchart on pp.10-11 to determine if the child or young person you're thinking about might need this kind of support. To support you to think through the meaning of *functioning,* please consider the following aspects of what *healthy functioning* might look like, when you're responding to the questions with him or her in mind.

Healthy functioning might include being:

- Physically well most of the time
- Able to learn and work
- Able to relax and play
- Able to sleep peacefully
- Responsible for themselves, others and things
- Able to have a consistent friendship group
- Able to seek help when needed
- Able to be alone
- Able to move through conflict to resolution
- Able to recover quickly if stressed
- Able to manage transitions relatively well
- Able to have a coherent sense of who they are and their story to date
- Able to express themselves clearly
- Able to use an emotional vocabulary

Creating Team Pupil

Once it is identified that a pupil needs a **Team Pupil** around them, the next thing is to think about who would be best placed for the individual pupil to have on their **Team**. The **Team** needs to be made up of those who work in the Key Pupil's school. This is not a multi-agency or network team (which might include social workers, CAMHS and so on), even though there may be a need for those teams and meetings too, in some cases. This **Team Pupil** is, in effect, like a family system brought together within the context of the bigger system called school, to be an important part of

Team Pupil in school

Providing the Team Pupil/Key Adult approach for pupils:
deciding interventions

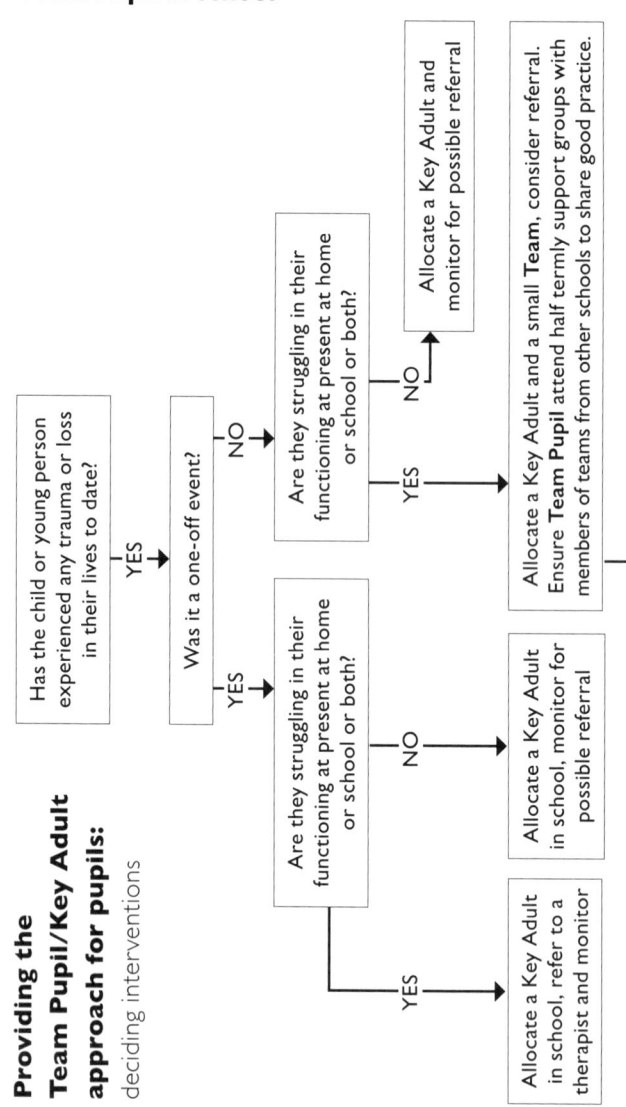

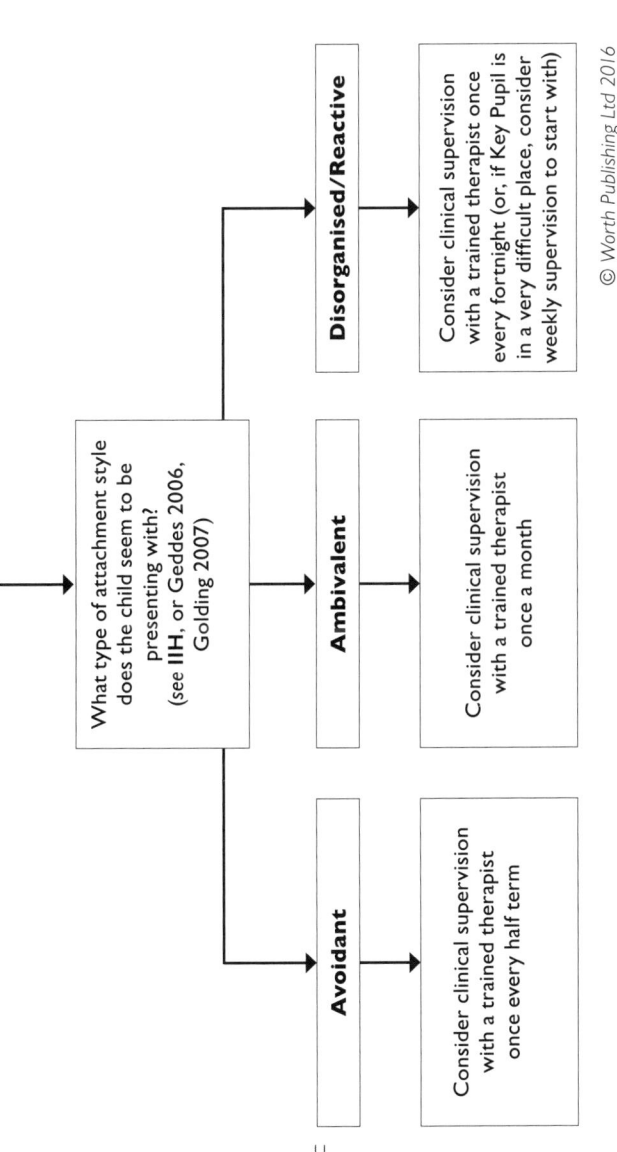

Team Pupil in school

the recovery process of the Key Pupil. The gender mix in the **Team** will need consideration, and please see p.14 and pp.22-3 for what else to bear in mind when selecting staff.

Let's find the best possible staff to be matched to these particular pupils in school. If we get our matches right, **Team Pupil** will be a cost-effective intervention that supports our pupils' recovery over time. These are the roles they will be playing (*and for time allocation issues, please see* p.34).

The key people in Team Pupil
KEY ADULT

Key Adults are usually members of support staff - teaching assistants (TAs), individual needs assistants (INAs), emotional literacy support assistants (ELSAs) or mentors from the main school staff. Key Adults prepare themselves to be the best additional attachment figures they can be for those pupils who have experienced **toxic stress** from pregnancy onwards, and/or have had compromised or disrupted relationships/connections with adults in their early years. Key Adults who are physically and emotionally present, empathic and attuned, provide the ground for these children and young people to thrive, supporting them into new learning, development and opportunities. In some **Teams**, there will also be a back-up adult who can step in when the Key Adult needs a break from this intense work.

The choice of the Key Adult (*see* **KAiS**) is the most important one to be made, as they really are on the frontline in terms of relationship recovery (*and see* **IIH** *for more reflections on who to choose*). The choice of back-up adult is also significant, so use similar criteria to those used for the Key Adult for this selection.

KEY TEACHER(S)

Key Teachers are drawn from classroom teachers, subject teachers, individual support teachers, nurture group teachers, tutors and form tutors. As part of **Team Pupil**, their role is to lead the way in terms of how learning is presented for a particular troubled pupil. They are inspirational leaders in either general learning or a particular subject area, holding the focus on the Key Pupil's areas of strengths and gifts, as well as modelling a passion for learning. Key Teachers spot opportunities to extend the Key Pupil's exploratory system, so that the pupil can begin to take the risks required in learning and then discover how energising and liberating doing so can be. Key Teachers may have a particularly lovely approach to the Key Pupil, or been observed engaging in a meaningful way, or perhaps unlocking their gifts through how they relate to the pupil, and teach.

SENIOR MANAGER(S)

The Senior Manager takes the lead in the formation and growth of **Team Pupil**. Responsiblities will vary from making a good match between Key Adult and pupil, through

Team Pupil in school

to freeing up staff to spend quality time with pupils in their care, to advocacy in the wider school community. The role of the Senior Manager is varied, meaning a range of skills is necessary. The troubled pupils need to experience the Senior Manager as 'big' enough, wise enough, kind enough and strong enough to 'hold them' psychologically (**Circle of Security®**, *see* **Glossary**), so it will be someone who is not fazed by the rollercoaster ride that can come as a result of getting close to trauma, secure enough not to engage in power dynamics within school, and who can be warm and playful. These pupils have often had an overdose of power, authority and control to their detriment, and the Senior Manager needs to facilitate different kinds of experiences for these pupils, especially in the area of discipline. As discipline is really all about learning, the Senior Manager can set the tone and pace of how and when that learning takes place.

Other considerations

In primary: the class teacher, SENCO/INCO and Assistant Head/Head teacher will probably already be in place in **Team Pupil**. However, if you are in a bigger school with multiple form entry, there may be two assistant heads and/or other support staff. If so, do use the criteria above to make a good match for the particular Key Pupil.

In secondary: the form tutor, SENCO/INCO and Head of Year will probably already be in position and there may not be much flexibility here. However, there will be flexibility for the subject teacher who can also form part of **Team Pupil**. This person needs to be picked based on the pupil's area of strength and interest - their resilience. Pick who you think will encourage and motivate the pupil further in terms of deepening their interest in this subject. You are essentially looking for a first-class role model.

In both primary and secondary, please consider having the school therapist or counsellor as part of **Team Pupil**. They can provide very helpful insights and reflections and take the team to another level in terms of supporting recovery.

Finally, if you've been asked to play one of the roles in **Team Pupil**, you can consider this a real honour, as you have been identified as someone who could make a real difference in the life of a child or young person. You'll be contributing particular skills, strengths, knowledge and expertise, and above all you'll be bringing yourself to this work. Because to be in **Team Pupil** is to offer your Key Pupil genuine relationship.

So not only will you be attachment aware and trauma informed (*see below*), but you'll be someone who knows that using PACE in all your interactions (*playfulness, acceptance, curiosity* and *empathy*, Hughes 2009, *and see below* p.68) is essential to enable children and young people to experience felt safety, and through rich relational experiences with you,

Team Pupil in school

and a mixture of nurture and challenge, to thrive. This is such rewarding and valuable work. Not only will the pupils benefit from having you in **Team Pupil**, but you will benefit too, however long it takes to know and feel that.

A NOTE ABOUT CONSULTATION

Each of us needs to be clear as to the boundaries of our role and responsibilities. There are occasions when attachment aware interventions will not be sufficient, and a trauma informed practitioner will need to be involved for specialist assessments, advice and interventions (*and see below* pp.39-41).

Who should that individual be? I would strongly recommend a specialist therapist with complex trauma/developmental trauma expertise. Our children and young people need appropriate professionals involved who will provide an extension to the ground work already laid down within the attachment aware practices employed in school. This is our joint ethical responsibility. As well as detailed assessments and direct interventions, these same professionals can also provide specialist supervision to staff in school on a regular basis. Increasing staff care increases our care-giving capacity, which means that we will then be more able to facilitate the permanency our pupils need. By facilitating and honouring the vehicle of relationship, we will be 'respecting biology' (Perry, 2104).

Let the quality connections begin!

Team Pupil in school

Attachment aware and trauma informed support for those who are hurting in schools

(drawing on the Seguridad model used by TouchBase™ © theyellowkite.co.uk)

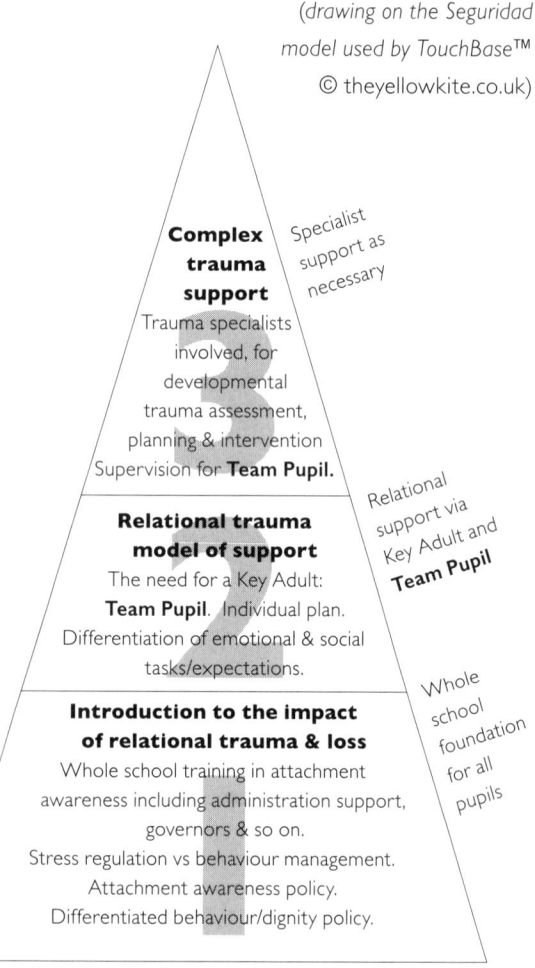

Complex trauma support
Trauma specialists involved, for developmental trauma assessment, planning & intervention
Supervision for **Team Pupil.**

Specialist support as necessary

Relational trauma model of support
The need for a Key Adult: **Team Pupil**. Individual plan. Differentiation of emotional & social tasks/expectations.

Relational support via Key Adult and **Team Pupil**

Introduction to the impact of relational trauma & loss
Whole school training in attachment awareness including administration support, governors & so on.
Stress regulation vs behaviour management.
Attachment awareness policy.
Differentiated behaviour/dignity policy.

Whole school foundation for all pupils

Part One

Becoming an effective Team Pupil

This book supports the members of **Team Pupil** to know their roles and the responsibilities attached, understanding where the boundaries lie between. You will all have done some attachment awareness training I hope (for at least two days) and perhaps also been involved with upskilling yourself around trauma and neuroscience so that you are in the best and most informed state to support your Key Pupil. It's helpful if you are familiar with the key principles from **IIH, WAM** and **STL**, as I refer to these books throughout the Series. These principles form the backdrop for everything you'll be doing. It will also be extremely helpful if you can read the other pocket books in the **Attachment Aware School Series**, so you can have a clear idea of what each **Team** member is responsible for and what their core aims are, in order to see how every member of **Team Pupil** holds important parts of the jigsaw, how you overlap and can interrelate.

Team Pupil in school

You will also need to know each other's boundaries really well so that if someone were to stray outside them, they would be able to clearly explain what they thought their responsibilities were and why they thought that action was important. There are sometimes many difficulties in our schools created unintentionally by staff *not* holding their boundaries or speaking up for themselves. You'll have a commitment to building trust within **Team Pupil**, respecting each other's experience and views, and communicating well both within your **Team** (*see* p.32, 37, 41) and with those outside the team (other staff and external agencies) (*see* p.48). You'll have a clear sense of what the expectations of **Team Pupil** are, as well as what you can expect by way of support and how you fit into the **Pyramid** of attachment aware and trauma informed support for your Key Pupil (*see above*). And lastly, and by no means least, you'll all be wanting to arrange that first, all-important meeting with the parent and carer of your Key Pupil, to introduce yourselves, meet and learn about each other and begin the important work of of supporting their child, your Key Pupil, together.

Core aims of Team Pupil

Team Pupil's aims are to

1. Support the pupil's sense of belonging and being known within a large setting where there are many transitions

2. Provide a sense of stability and security to those who have experienced disruption and impermanency

3. Provide a family structure in school for those who are still learning what family is

4. Work in collaboration with parents and carers

5. Create a smaller world for those who have experienced too many transitions

6. Create a sense of predictability when there is so much change going on in a school system

Team Pupil in school

7 Support the pupil to develop a sense of feeling connected and not alone, despite school feeling like a 'Big Ask' in the midst of what they have lived or are going through right now

Ideal qualities of Team Pupil members

Cares for self, fit ☆ Dedicated ☆ Loyal

Together ☆ Consistent ☆ Flexible

Patient ☆ Warm ☆ Determined ☆ Kind

Grounded ☆ Creative ☆ Relational

Great team players

Open minded ☆ Still learning ☆ Well regulated

Highly emotionally literate

Perservering ☆ Committed

Gentle with their strength, strong

with their gentleness

Relational ☆ Hope bearers ☆ Advocates

Dreamers of the day!

PLEASE ALSO CONSIDER THE FOLLOWING WHEN CHOOSING TEAM PUPIL MEMBERS:

- Presentation style
- Gender
- Communication style
- Interests
- Hobbies/Skills/Strengths
- Commitment
- Career plan - likely to stay in post for the forseeable future
- Resolution of their own trauma, loss, grief
- Likes and appreciates the child or young person!
- Where possible, is already liked by the pupil

Good questions about how Team Pupil works in practice

↪ *How will our **Team** know we are making a difference?*

As I'll be describing later on (p.55) it's helpful to map out your Key Pupil's recovery times around low level stressors in school. You should see their stress responses change in a positive direction over time. You should see them wanting to be closer to you (seeking proximity) rather than relying solely on themselves - allowing themselves to show some dependency. You should see also evidence of the pupil extending themselves out of their comfort zone - having a go

Team Pupil in school

at activities that previously they might have been too anxious to try. Remember that when their **attachment system** is well attended to, as you'll all be doing (especially the Key Adult), their **exploratory system** will be able to kick in.

↪ *Some staff might need to change in **Team Pupil** because of sickness, maternity leave and so on. What happens then?*

There are uncertainties in life. We can only do our absolute best to create teams of those who set off to support your Key Pupil over the long term, that is over a minimum of two to three years. However, life happens. When people have to move on, please ensure you create a really good ending. Some of these pupils might never have had a good ending before. They may have had people come and go with no explanation, no support, no understanding of the grief caused. This time around, give him or her a different experience. Ensure you have space to look back over your journey together with your Key Pupil. Create a memory book and facilitate some ending rituals, for example, sharing cards, sharing a cake, swapping small gifts … the more time and attention you invest in an ending, into a goodbye and a hello, the more likely these pupils are to transition well. They need supportive scaffolding to manage transitions, especially because they have all 'lost' people along the way. Many pupils who have experienced **relational trauma** and loss are grieving, and not many people recognise this.

↳ *How should we respond to parents of other pupils who request a **Team Pupil** for their child?*

Ensure you have created a school policy that includes attachment aware and trauma informed interventions and when you use them. You are more likely to have difficulties if you are not explicit about who these are for and why. Remember (*and see* p.5) that these teams are set up for those who have experienced **relational trauma** or loss and are showing developmental vulnerabilities at home, or school, or both. Use the Flowchart from pp.10-11 in your policy.

↳ *How do we respond to Ofsted about the amount of time given to being in **Team Pupil**?*

Ensure you are clear in your own mind about the journey of recovery these pupils need. Ensure you have a clear policy in school documenting what you do and why you do it. Use this Series for the detail. Ensure you are capturing the pupil's narratives through case studies. Use your time with Ofsted to educate them about the impact of **relational trauma** and loss: many will appreciate your wisdom and insight. Remember the work of the Consortium of Emotional Well Being and the different documents out now that recommend attachment aware and trauma informed practice in schools (*see* **References, Useful documents**)

Team Pupil in school

↪ *What if other staff undermine what **Team Pupil** are trying to do by getting directly involved and using other strategies that are not attachment aware and trauma informed?*

Take a deep breath. Focus on being grounded and re-group with the rest of **Team Pupil** as soon as possible. Decide who is best to gently challenge this person. Give them the benefit of the doubt, as they may not even be aware of what they are doing. Sadly many adults struggle with self awareness! It may be that they're quick to apologise and change their position. If they don't, you will need to take this difficulty higher. Your school have invested in you as **Team Pupil**. Anything that undermines this investment will cost the school in many ways, so it's important that this problem is flagged up sooner rather than later (*and see* pp.48-52).

↪ *What should we do if we want to establish a **Team Pupil**, but the Head is not supportive?*

Not all staff will have had sufficient training YET, and so please bear with those who are still on that journey. Slowly, slowly use opportunities to raise awareness, to educate. If possible, encourage the Head to meet up with another Head or an Attachment Lead from another school where there is attachment aware and trauma informed work going on. For example use the Attachment Lead Network website to find out who is near you! (*see* **Useful Contacts**) Keep persevering. It is only a matter of time and everyone will realise that we have been overlooking something very significant for so many years in education - the power of relationship.

↳ *What should we do if the pupil's carer or parent is not comfortable with their child having a **Team Pupil**?*

In my experience this does not happen often but I have had one or two Key Adults turn up at support groups 'incognito', so to speak, as sadly the parents are in denial about how needful of support their child is. Please be compassionate and remember that there are folk out there grieving for the children they didn't have, and for the new tomorrows that they didn't plan. There is so much grief around in fostering and adoption - not just for the children and young people themselves, but for the birth parents, the foster carers, the special guardians and the adoptive parents. And there is much trauma and loss, as I've found as I've journeyed with different families over the years. Go gently. Build relationship. Build trust. Slowly, slowly, you will be able to share your concerns and be heard. If there are really no shifts and you are even experiencing confrontation, then in some situations the leadership team will need to sit down and have a frank conversation; we can't honour our ethical duty of care to those in our schools if we cannot engage in this type of support work. It may be that a referral needs to be made to social services at this point to flag up your concern, as this then becomes a safeguarding matter.

Team Pupil in school

↳ *What can I do as a parent, if my child's school says it can't or won't provide a Key Adult or **Team Pupil**?*

I would first check out whether the school has had any attachment awareness and trauma informed training. Usually schools are doing the best they can with what they know. My guess would be that a school that says this hasn't had this kind of training, so as a starter might be to suggest they check out our Attachment Lead Network website (*see* p.95) for training opportunities or suggest other training providers in this specialist area. Or you could show them what you're reading (especially *Inside I'm Hurting* (2007) and the **Attachment Aware School Series**), and say you'd like your child to be supported through the Key Adult/**Team Pupil** approach.

Please note that even scarce resources can't excuse a school from providing a stable relationship for your child with an adult in school. I know of one committed school who are struggling a lot financially but who realise that in their catchment area there are many, many pupils who have developmental vulnerabilities and attachment difficulties and need Key Adults. Together we came up with the idea of every member of staff employed by the school being allocated a pupil/pupils to key work, even the Head and the caretaker! Why not?

Other schools may choose to bring in long-term volunteers from charities such as the education charity TLG (Transforming Lives for Good, *see* **Useful Contacts**). Creativity is sometimes needed in the 'how,' but one way or the other we have to pave a way to honour relationship.

Schools like the one above know there isn't a choice if they are to reach 'the unreachables' and help them settle. Let's get this Key Adult/**Team Pupil** idea fully embedded into school culture!

But if the school is reluctant, ask if they are willing to invest in *relationships that last*, and recognise how important this is for pupils who have been wounded 'in relationship'. You can tell a lot about a school by who and what they invest in. What are the priorities? What will they do if the going gets tough? Do they have a zero tolerance approach, or are they determined to practice inclusion on every level?

You can play a significant part in raising awareness of the importance of protecting a relationship with an adult in school. If your child has been wounded in relationship - relationships will be the vehicle back towards adaption and recovery. And how does this school look after their staff? Do the staff have a Key Adult approach? Do they have access to support groups? If not, would you be able to work with the staff to introduce some of these ideas?

Team Pupil in school

Sadly, most teacher training doesn't include much on child development, attachment, neuroscience or trauma - yet. The Consortium of Emotional Well Being in schools is trying its best to advocate for this! (*see* **Useful Contacts**).

Whatever you do, please remember there are many staff out there with pupils who have experience of **relational trauma** and loss, working in schools in the ways I describe, amazed and delighted with how their Key Pupil has responded, how much safer and supported the child or young person evidently feels, how their learning has progressed. The comments we receive are so moving.

Part Two

The attachment aware, trauma informed Team Pupil in practice

If **Team Pupil** works well you are onto a winner in school! So what can help? Choosing the right team is the foundation stone, based on the roles and responsibilities I described earlier and in each of the pocket books in the **Attachment Aware School Series**. Enthusiasm and commitment are also vital ingredients, of course. However, what is critical at all times is excellent communication.

Team Pupil in school

Responsibilities of Team Pupil

▷ Trust each member of **Team Pupil** as equals, and support each other, recognising that 'we are all in this together'
▷ Check in with your Key Pupil on a daily or weekly basis dependent on your role in the team
▷ Use PACE in all interactions with the pupil (*see* **STL** *and below*, p.68)
▷ Contribute to and work to the Individual Development Plan (IDP) created for your Key Pupil
▷ Provide rich, relational opportunities in order for the pupil to thrive
▷ Keep the parent/carer in the loop
▷ Contain the heightened anxiety of the child or young person which can often get projected out into the wider system of school
▷ Model what healthy grown-ups can look like
▷ Practice strengthening your Key Pupil's areas of developmental vulnerability in a safe way
▷ Recognise the nature of the 'Big Ask' of these pupils in our schools (*see* p.56)
▷ Give the pupil opportunity to experience safety, regulation and joy
▷ Create opportunity to relate to the child or young person at their emotional or social age rather than their chronological age

- Give the pupil breathers in what could be quite an intense process for them, being educated by grown-ups, whom they don't trust
- Refer to each other if there are difficulties or successes
- Provide feedback to each other on your Key Pupil's stressors and calmers
- Support and cheer the pupil along as we know these children and young people can have poorer outcomes than their peers
- Celebrate successes!
- Keep the parent/ carer informed regarding activities or curriculum content that might trigger feelings regarding loss
- Monitor the plans for the Key Pupil, updating as and when necessary
- Liaise with external agencies and know when to refer the Key Pupil for more specialist trauma informed support or therapy
- Continue to upskill yourselves in terms of attachment awareness and trauma informed practice
- Participate in supervision and support groups with others doing similar work
- Be prepared to demonstrate to Ofsted how the work is supporting the pupils' engagement in school, and to share understanding of why the pupil might have a 'spikey profile'
- Advocate for attachment aware/trauma informed practice within the wider school system

Team Pupil in school

Determining the time to be allocated

I am often asked about how much time should be allocated within each of these roles. Obviously this varies from pupil to pupil, but I will give you some pointers so that you can think about what might work best for the individual child or young person in your care. Before I outline these pointers, it's a good opportunity to think together about quality moments. So much of the support we give can be made up of moments like these, and they will probably mean more than we ever realise.

Quality moments

In busy, fast paced schools it can often feel like everyone is rushing about, passing you by. For a child or young person who already has a sense of 'not belonging', of being on the fringes, of being overlooked or maybe even misunderstood, school can be such a 'Big Ask'. Every now and then consider pressing the pause button, stopping, breathing deeply - being fully present. Be aware of your body posture. Use your body to support you to become more open, warm and approachable.

Greet the pupil you're working with, using their name, and welcome them with a smile. Listen, really listen. Use your eyes as well as your ears to listen. These children and young people tell us so much more non-verbally about what is going on for them. Behaviour is communication. Affirm or paraphrase what they share. There are many possible moments. Make sure you seize them. Quality moments at various times throughout a school day or week will speak louder than you will ever imagine. These children will remember. They are watching. They notice.

So now let's think about more formal time, which will be determined by the Senior Manager in collaboration with the others in **Team Pupil**.

TIME AND SUPPORT

I always advocate for at least 30 minutes per week of undivided attention with a pupil. This is the minimum level of support and will not be adequate for the majority of our pupils who have experienced **relational trauma** and loss. Let's consider some questions to ask before determining their support hours.

- ▷ Is there any risky behaviour or talk?
- ▷ Are they clingy?
- ▷ Are they stuck in their developmental or learning progress?
- ▷ Do you feel like you know them or do they seem quite hidden?
- ▷ Is home reporting big difficulties?
- ▷ Does the pupil use different handwriting styles, voices and personas?
- ▷ Do you see evidence of self-harm?
- ▷ Does the pupil run off and hide?

Team Pupil in school

▷ Does the pupil leave the site or find it difficult to come in?
▷ Are you nearing a big transition and do they find transition hard?

If any of the above are true, then I would strongly recommend you increase the level of support in place. Be aware that there are some pupils out there who will need 25 hours of support per week. Note I use the word *support*, not someone as a minder or a monitor - support. Someone to be a fellow traveller so that this pupil does not remain pseudo-independent but starts to realise that they are not alone, that it is OK to let others in, and to trust. It is only when they can allow themselves to take this risk that they will be fully in a position to settle to learn and make the most of everything on offer to them in our schools. Please also check out the pocket book for Senior Manager (**SMiS**, p.20), for more on time allocation.

*Time with the **Key Pupil**:* So the time allocated will depend on how much support the pupil needs, determined by their attachment style, their behaviour presentation and the risks around for him or her at a particular time (*and see Flowchart on* pp.10-11). It is also hoped that the **Team** will check in on the pupil daily/weekly as individuals, and together about once a month (but just for a quick hello and reminder that you are all there behind the scenes working together, on the pupil's side to help them be all they can be!) Remember this work is based on knowing your individual Key Pupil through attunement, and so all these timings are just baselines and are not intended to replace your attentiveness, attunement and responsiveness. No text book can guide this, only knowing the pupil themselves will determine what you as a **Team** decide to do.

Time with each other as a team: **Team Pupil** also needs to have time built in to connect with one another. It's not enough to simply have a quick word running past each other in the carpark, or in the corridor on the way to work with someone else, or another class, or to attend to another task. You may need to experiment with which forms of communication are best and when the times are in which two or all of you can be most focused. But let's figure that out together, rather than settling for less. These children deserve our best care and consideration, and not just when we are in front of them but when we are discussing what's happening for them behind the scenes too. As a baseline, once every half term is a minimum requirement.

Please bear in mind that straight after school is not ideal for any meeting! And please consider the need to process the day and to take a comfort break to refuel before expecting any kind of meeting. If I'm asked to go and talk to a staff team after school, I insist we have refreshments first. If we want our children to experience rich, relational interventions we need to also value our staff team's needs too. The 3 R's (*see below*) are also important for adults.

Team Pupil in school

Some possible ideas to reflect on, *in the following order*:

1 **Regulate** *for example*
- share some food (crunchy/citrus to wake us up!)
- have a drink, or sip water
- swim, stretch
- toilet
- change of space
- exercise, walk
- hand cream, lip balm
- mindfulness …

2 **Relate** *check in with each other, play a quick game, time to talk, for example -*
- about weekend
- forthcoming holiday
- play Top Five (card game) to deepen knowledge of one another and build relationship …

3 **Reason**
- reflective practice
- problem solving
- creating plans
- sharing thinking …

As I mentioned earlier, good practice is linked to staff care and welfare as there is a direct correlation between the way staff are looked after and supported and their care-giving capacity. As well as attending to our own stress levels and the corporate stress in our schools (*see* **STL**) a school seeking to be attachment aware and trauma informed will ensure that each member of staff has their own Key Adult, access to half termly or termly support groups, and access to clinical supervision on a regular basis for our work with children and young people who are presenting with complex trauma symptoms. This is ethically responsible practice.

Providing a Pyramid of attachment aware and trauma informed support

It is important to note here that when I first set out in my work in this specialist area within education, I wanted to see staff empowered to realise the difference we could make, whatever our role or responsibility within school. Every relationship has the power to confirm or challenge all that's gone on before. It was never my intention to suggest that we didn't need trauma experts involved. A good school does not go it alone, it forfeits its pride on behalf of its children's best interests and reaches out to those who know more about the complexity associated with trauma as and when it needs to. We all bring different contributions to the overall recovery process. It's not a 'them or us' dynamic. It's about us all complementing each other's skills, strengths and aptitudes, to give our pupils the best possible chance to settle to learn and to make the most of everything on offer in our schools and in their lives. So let's have a think about when and how to involve trauma experts.

Team Pupil in school

Basic attachment awareness greatly complements the work of a school for all children (*see* Level 1 of the **Pyramid** on p.18), but children who have been traumatised need more than this, hence our development of the model outlined in the **Attachment Aware School Series** with the creation of **Team Pupil** and the Key Adult relationship, with parents in partnership (Level 2). When the going gets really tough, the school will also need to involve external professionals who are experienced in working therapeutically with children who have experienced **relational trauma** and loss (Level 3). These children need a very different type of care compared to their peers because of everything they have experienced, culminating in **toxic stress**. I don't think we should ever underestimate the level of pain many of these children have lived through and are still carrying.

So the piece that is missing all too often for the children we are focused on in schools is a knowledge of trauma and its impact. Your Key Pupil has been traumatised in some way, and so will need interventions that support recovery. Such interventions may well be a lifeline in terms of their capacity to function at home, at school and in the wider community. We all have a duty of care to ensure this.

Contacting trauma specialists

Wise members of **Team Pupil** know that they need to stay connected with external professionals who have specialist skills and expertise, who can carry out assessments, develop individual development plans, provide consultation and supervision, and run support groups or reflective spaces, as the need arises (Stage 3 of the **Pyramid**). Anyone in the **Team** can raise their concerns about a possible need for referral, as can the parent or carer of the Key Pupil you are working with and they are living with.

This work need to be carried out by those with therapy backgrounds or close clinical supervision from therapists, since these children have experienced significant **relational trauma** and loss. **Attachment Leads** can pave the way by helping schools choose the right kinds of support from all the services out there. The Senior Manager or school counsellor in **Team Pupil** may be best placed to develop links with them prior to the need for specialists arising.

I strongly recommend selecting professionals who have a background in Theraplay and DDP, specialist trauma interventions that can positively impact recovery especially for those in the fostering and adoption world (*please see websites for further information, see* **Useful Contacts**).

Working well within Team Pupil

Forming **Team Pupil** will mean learning to work well together over time. You'll need to encourage and support each other, learn from each other, find out where your roles stop and start. As I mentioned earlier, you'll need to be clear about where your boundaries are with each other, and

Team Pupil in school

sometimes you'll need to assert those boundaries with each other. I don't mean we should be going around squaring up to others, claiming our territory! Simply that we need to sometimes use gentle challenge to wonder about why things are as they are, exploring how to go forward together, rather than merely carrying on upset, thinking it's not worth it, not speaking to each other or at worse, having a big conflict over it. We are working as professionals. It is our duty of care to our pupils that we communicate respectfully and well to and with one another. Consider every difficulty as an opportunity to develop even better quality practice.

Be aware how powerful fear can be, and fear does get stirred up sometimes in our work with children and young people who have experienced **relational trauma** and loss. When you sense yourself feeling a bit out of control and the anxiety associated with this, check in on your fear levels. Sometimes we express our fear in ways that are not helpful, because sadly, fear can motivate many different defensive behaviours.

I've encountered this so often amongst the pupils I work with, but my puppy Maisie has also taught me a lot! The other day I accidentally trapped her lead in the door of my office as I was entering with her. She was so alarmed by this that she suddenly became out of control and out of character, jumping up at me, growling and barking and as if she might bite me (but I knew she wouldn't). Immediately I went into reassurance mode, talking gently and softly, repeatedly telling her that she was OK. After a few seconds more, I started to stroke her really gently, repeating my words. Very quickly she recovered. Her heart beat slowed down, her posture relaxed and she started wagging her tail, as if forgetting what had just happened!

Remember Maisie when you are alarmed or if someone you are caring for is alarmed. Good practice doesn't meet fear head on with defensive actions, including withdrawal: but moves into a different mode to be physically and emotionally available, to attune, to respond and to attend to.

And this applies to each other, as adults, just as much as to the children and young people we work with. In **Team Pupil** we need to guard against 'acting out' the displaced fear that may get stirred up amongst us because of the trauma of working alongside traumatised pupils, and the resulting potential for **splitting** (blaming and taking sides). We need to be gentle, empathic and open with ourselves and each other in this work, and seek support when we need it from trauma experts. We need to know when to ask for help, just as much as we hope our Key Pupils will learn to do!

Attachment aware and trauma informed practice, not behaviourist responses

Good practice in an attachment aware and trauma informed school will mean managing great stress and shame regulation on behalf of its pupils. There are some children and young

Team Pupil in school

people who could actually become more distressed if we were to use behaviourist practices, logic, cause and effect type work because these pupils are too fragile internally and don't have sufficient neural pathways in their pre-frontal cortex. Instead of teaching them, we can end up aggravating them. I'm sure you, like me, want to see a reduction in the numbers of exclusions across primary and secondary phases. These children and young people don't need more of the same, dressed up with different names. They need something different. If you have evidence now of something not working, switch your intervention! (*and see the chart comparing approaches* on the following pages).

Please bear in mind that those children who seem to be stuck, who don't seem to be 'getting it' using the usual discipline policies, need us to provide alternatives within our schools. Note that I say 'within our schools', not somewhere else! These children need us to do all we can to keep things as stable as possible. In fact, these children need us to ensure they can continue to be around familiar staff, in their familiar contexts for as long as they can be. Your school might be the most permanency they have ever experienced. Please don't give up just because it is hard work. That is the nature of trauma. It is a rollercoaster ride! Come on board and I can guarantee this will be the most rewarding work you will ever do if you truly stick it out. Together, as part of an effective **Team Pupil**, which keeps itself emotionally regulated and stable as well.

Home/School partnership

We now realise that we need parents and carers on board with our teams! Some of us should probably apologise for having kept them at arm's length over the years. The adoptive parents, carers and special guardians out there have a wealth of knowledge and experience in the area of trauma. Why? Because they have lived it with their child or teenager and have usually tried many different approaches already. Why would we not want to join up? Many are also receiving advice from trauma experts through reading, training events, parent/carer support groups, assessments, consultations and therapy contexts, for example through DDP (*see* **References**).

Together you can support the child or young person they are living with and you are working with move from having a *fragile* sense of self to becoming more robust, with an *integrated* sense of self. Together you can support this pupil to move from having *poor internal controls* to learning *self-control*. Both these relational attributes can be passed on to these pupils by them having repeated experience of particular types of relational interactions. They need you to facilitate them to be all they should have been first time round. For these children and young people to thrive, they really need us. We are all needed, and are a vital part of the recovery journey.

Find out more about the benefits and challenges of home/school partnership in **IIH**, (Chapter 12), **WAM** (Chapter 16) and check out an example of our Home School Partnership

Team Pupil in school

ATTACHMENT AWARE AND TRAUMA INFORMED APPROACH IN SCHOOL

Facilitating relative dependency

Creating emotional safety through sensitive attuned care

Becoming stress managers

The adult being responsible for holding boundaries

Flexibility of approach

Focussing on strengthening a pupil's internal controls

Encouraging relational proximity - time in for the pupil

Being responsive

Being preventative

Expectations and tasks based on emotional and social age of pupil

Adapting the environment to the pupil

All transitions to be identified and prepared for

Accountability for the processes used by education staff

Using the pupil's history so far as a framework in which to interpret behaviour

Strengthening a pupil's sense of self

Using relational influence to create motivation

Attending to the attachment needs of the pupil

VS BEHAVIOURAL APPROACH

vs	**encouraging further pseudo independence**
vs	the use of more authority, power, control
vs	**managing behaviour**
vs	more consequences for the pupil
vs	**rigidity of approach**
vs	imposing external controls that the pupil might not be developmentally ready for yet
vs	**relational withdrawal or distance - time out for the pupil**
vs	being reactive
vs	**being crisis driven**
vs	expectations and tasks being matched to the pupil's chronological age
vs	**expecting the pupil to adapt to the existing environment**
vs	only identifying the major transitions that a pupil might face
vs	**only accountability for performance/outcome of pupils**
vs	blank canvass approach
vs	**assuming the pupil is robust enough to manage everyday opportunities and stressors**
vs	the use of rewards and sanctions to create motovation
vs	**assuming all attachment needs have been met**

Developed from Forbes 2012, p.178 for the UK education system

Team Pupil in school

review sheet at the back of **STL** (*and please read* **PCiS** *in the* **Attachment Aware School Series**, *the pocket book for parents and carers*).

Relating to other members of the school community

Sometimes our colleague are really supportive. Often they know a lot about attachment awareness and trauma informed practice themselves, they are interested in what **Team Pupil** is doing, and keep to their own role with respect and thoughtfulness. These colleagues are invaluable!

However, sometimes there are difficulties in our schools created (unintentionally) by other staff not holding their boundaries; or, unfortunately, sometimes intentionally. When this happens **Team Pupil** will need to speak up for themselves. As all of us know who have been part of school communities, there are all sorts of people out there who we will come into contact with whilst part of **Team Pupil**. I will outline some advice on how to engage with each 'type'!

☺ *The supporter*
This is someone who loves what you are part of and doing.

Possible contribution Ensure you connect in with this person regularly. You are going to need some encouragement along the way as these pupils often have spikey profiles in terms of progress.

Possible risk Supporters may inadvertently interfere and cross over boundaries with the pupils in your care, even though their motivation is likely to be well-intentioned. You will need to be very clear, holding your boundaries and affirming to the person that you welcome their support and that their role is to provide encouragement to you, not to get involved.

🙁 *The cynic*

This is someone who rolls their eyes as they see you and the pupil coming down the corridor, maybe even sighing or muttering as if what you are doing is a waste of time, to get directly involved.

Possible contribution They have noticed you are doing something different! Well done! You are challenging their perception. See if you can utilise moments here and there to educate this person. The scientific facts usually go down well. Swot up on the neuroscience around trauma (Sunderland 2016).

Possible risk If you are feeling discouraged anyway, this type of response may feed your discouragement. Be wary of spending too much time with them whilst they hold this view. Instead, place yourself around those who do 'get it'.

Team Pupil in school

☹ *The saboteur*

This is someone who seems to undermine what you do with the pupil: maybe talks over you, uses their power and influence to get the pupil to undertake something different to what you have set up ...

Possible contribution There is some kind of interest in this pupil, rather than them being completely overlooked. Use this to your advantage by passing on snippets of information to this person so they stay updated.

Possible risk This could seriously affect your relationship with your pupil, reflecting badly on you, especially if the pupil feels you don't have any influence or say, as they could quickly feel unsafe around you. The pupil needs to know you are big enough, strong enough, wise enough and kind enough so that you can position yourself as their additional attachment figure in school. So be protective. First ask for a meeting to discuss your concerns. If this doesn't go well, involve the Senior Manager in **Team Pupil** and take it higher if necessary. Keep going until this dynamic shifts. And remember that behaving destructively probably indicates that this person is probably feeling threatened and needs some support for themselves. Behaviour is communication!

The smoother(er)!

This is someone who is too nurturing with the pupil you are supporting. Someone who may have their own difficulties to attend to from either the past or present.

Possible contribution Many of the pupils we support
	with teams have huge nurture deficits: some have
	lived in relationally deprived contexts. It is great
	that someone is responding to this need. At
	the same time, we may need to help them stay
	boundaried. It will help by stating what the plan is
	for this particular pupil.

Possible risk The adult and child could become
	enmeshed with one another adding to the
	complexities already around for the child. The
	pupils we focus in on in the **Attachment Aware
	School Series** need a careful balance of both
	nurture and gentle challenge. Not receiving
	gentle challenge could leave these pupils stuck
	developmentally as they need to take some risks
	in order to extend themselves and grow. Their
	insecure lens could also be colluded with, taking the
	unhelpful message away that you need someone
	focused just on you in order to get your needs met.
	A pupil emeshed with a member of staff may be
	unable to have a sense of separate-ness.

Team Pupil in school

 *The survivor*

This is someone who has had a difficult start in life themselves. They had to just get on and manage. They often feel bitter about the fact that possibly no-one ever noticed, cared or even tried to help. They are in fact still wounded and to date, have not experienced their own recovery. They will often make impatient or seemingly cold statements such as 'a good old hiding never did anyone any harm', 'they just need to get on with it' …

Possible contribution this person knows what it feels like to be in pain or to experience loss relationally. Be very kind and compassionate, knowing they are wounded. Comment on how all children have needs, and that some need the opposite of what they have already experienced.

Possible risk As with the saboteur, survivors could discourage you further if you are already discouraged and could undermine your work. Ensure you check in with one of your supportive colleagues after spending time with a survivor, whose behaviour has indicated they haven't had enough rich and empathic relationships themselves.

Celebrating progress!

Remember the *noticing out loud* technique I described in *Inside I'm Hurting* (2007)? Well, this can be used in order to mark areas that your Key Pupil is getting stronger in. For example: "*I notice that your trusting part is getting so much stronger as you are now able to ...*" Map out what you noticed when you first started working with them, and what you notice now.

Do consider collating the evidence of progress in concrete form through photos, signed post it notes, photocopies ... If something is healthy and appropriate, capture it somehow, anyone in **Team Pupil**! You will need to protect it, as this celebratory work will be sabotaged on days or at times when the pupil gets in touch with grief, which is so linked to his **relational trauma** and loss. Only use books and folders such as these when your Key Pupil is in a state of alert or calm. And keep watching, waiting and wondering on his behalf. Join up the dots for him, on his behalf.

Be very wary in all of this feedback that you do not over-use evaluation, since evaluation runs the risk of disabling - acceptance enables. Some pupils will only be able to manage little doses of praise. Even if they seem to enjoy it, watch their states during and after receiving feedback. Remember you are a stress regulator and so attention to their nervous system must be your priority. Pupils can't digest anything in a state of alarm, and so it will be time wasted if we're not using attunement first and foremost.

Team Pupil in school

Evidencing our work

At this time of close scrutiny in our schools where we are evaluated left, right and centre, it is important that we seize the opportunity to influence and educate others by maximising the use of case studies to evidence our work. In our Attachment Lead Network meetings around the country, we encourage the use of the Four Slide series to evidence our work. We ask those presenting to prepare a 20-30 minute presentation of four slides on -

i   the Key Pupil's **relational trauma** and loss
ii   presenting behaviours at the start of the intervention
iii   interventions used
iv   where the Key Pupil is now in terms of their presentation.

If we use this structure it helps all of us to stay focussed on what really matters - recovery. We are all in this work to support pupils to recover from **toxic stress**, to build healthy attachments to the grown-ups caring for them in school and to engage their exploratory systems so they can make the most out of their time in education. We are thinking together about their story to date, to determine whether we can see evidence of a more robust sense of self developing, not emotional collapse when experiencing stress. Evidence of internal controls strengthening. Evidence of pupils engaging in curriculum and enjoying achievement and success. Evidence that they are connected in and contributing.

Another good measure that I recommend is that of recovery time. At the beginning of our interventions the Key Pupil's stress presentation is documented (how he or she reacts when something sets off anxiety in him or her), as well as stress triggers. At various points we measure and record recovery times from stress. For the purpose of this exercise we just use ordinary, everyday school stressors, for example having a go at some work, needing to follow the lead of a grown-up and so on. It is remarkable how the recovery time shifts from sometimes hours to minutes!

There are also other measures that could benefit this work, including saliva tests measuring the level of cortisol at different points of the day (this could be arranged in collaboration with parents and with trauma specialists). It also needs to be said that in this type of work, trauma and its effects come and go over the life course and so there are no neat measures, so to speak. The pupils we work with go up and down with their progress in terms of their educational outcomes, thus presenting with spikey profiles in schools. It's hardly surprising when they have been wounded to the core and are left with developmental vulnerabilities and scars that take considerable time to heal. Let's recognise how huge the 'Big Ask' of wanting them to engage with school really is.

Team Pupil in school

The Big Ask in school

Being self- and other-aware in order to make wise choices   **FEELING SAFE**

Being free from toxic shame   **Having a feeling of belonging**

TRUSTING GROWN-UPS

Relinquishing some control to grown-ups   *Being freed up enough to engage in curiosity and exploration*

Being free from anxiety

FEELING SPECIAL AND SIGNIFICANT

Taking the risks required in learning

Following the lead of grown-ups

Negotiating key developmental stages such as adolescence   *Managing multiple transitions*

Managing sensory overload

We are aware that we are living in a culture that demands quick fixes. But we are alongside hurting pupils who will take time to process everything that has happened to them. Just as with the usual grieving process, there are a few stages pupils will need to move through in order to adapt and recover.

With all this in mind I am keen to see Ofsted start to measure what processes are in place for these pupils rather than only using very basic outcome measures. Schools need to be assessed on how they are effectively including those who engage in rejecting type behaviours, who have been wounded relationally, those who are on the fringes of our society ... there is a huge cost to our local communities and to our wider world when they are not included. An exclusion is never the final story. Relationships matter - enormously - for the health and wellbeing of EVERYONE. In fact, do check out those who are at the cutting edge of the work around these issues, including Dr Gabor Maté (*see* **References**). As you and I join up everything that's now known about the importance of attachment across the life span, we start to realise that connection, or the lack of connection, has a direct correlation on outcomes - for better or worse.

Team Pupil in school

10 things others say about the work of Team Pupil

> She is now in school. We used to have such a hard time keeping her there!
>
> *He knows where we are if he feels his alarm is going off, he comes to us.*
>
> She loves the picture of her team and keeps it firmly attached to her pencil case.
>
> *He beamed as soon as we told him he would have his own team - "Really?"*
>
> He seems to have a reason to be in school nowadays.
>
> *For the first time in a long while she has said that she likes school. That's progress!*
>
> Somehow the team seems to hold him, maybe it makes him feel safe?
>
> *It was as if we were all holding different parts of him, now we know what makes the whole of Jack!*
>
> It doesn't sound much, formalising a team around a child in school, but wow how powerful it seems to be.
>
> *In the past so much time was wasted with everyone getting involved. We are so much tighter now and more consistent in our practice. This is usually difficult in such a big school as ours, but seems so much easier now we have a team.*

Part Three

Facilitating the best outcomes

So, you and your colleagues have created **Team Pupil** together. Fantastic! You are on the road to supporting a pupil in your care into recovery. What a privilege and an honour! None of you may ever realise just how much of a difference having you alongside will make in this child or young person's life. Believe me: even if they don't appreciate you now or even do everything they can to reject you, remember that they will NEVER forget that all of you stood alongside. That you believed in them. That you valued their life and could see the potential of everything they could be. That you cared. They will take this knowledge and experience as parting gifts that will remain with them as constants.

Team Pupil in school

Someone else may see the full benefits of all your input later on, since for some pupils you will be some of the first adults to ever get alongside and be trusted with their life. For others you will have the rewarding experience of seeing them flourish, and become, whilst you know them, everything they should have been first time around.

Team Photograph

A significant part of the work of **Team Pupil** is to facilitate a sense of permanency for your Key Pupil, enabling him or her to develop a feeling that they are being 'kept in mind'. To support this, you need a photo of **Team Pupil**! If your Key Pupil is happy to be included too, invite them to join you for the picture. However, it will be just as helpful to have one of just the **Team** of adults. Your Key Pupil needs to have a copy. There also needs to be one up in a central place at home and one up in school somewhere, for example the classroom or Head of Year's room. It needs to be referred to regularly to remind your Key Pupil that they are being considered on a regular basis, that they are not (as they might think), 'lost from mind'.

To deepen this experience further, the whole of **Team Pupil** needs to check in together every now and then. It doesn't need to be for long but just a quick hello and a reminder that you are all behind the scenes championing this pupil, doing all you can to support them to make the most out of school. It's the fact that the pupil 'sees' you altogether that will be powerful. And do remember to use your Key Pupil's name when you say 'team'! Team Candy, Team Micah, Team Lee etc.

And please remember to make a note of significant dates like birthdays, Christmas, adoption day or moving day and so on, so you can all sign a card for him or her. These things may seem small. But they can have huge impact.

So - wow! What an amazing opportunity lies ahead of you. This section will address some of the key things to bear in mind together as you journey forward. Let's start with a short exercise as we've done in the individual pocket books

Team Pupil in school

(*see opposite*). You could do this together, or think about it separately and then share your responses together as part of getting to know each other and building your **Team**.

A HOLDING BOUNDARIES

What is a boundary?
As human beings we all need boundaries. Think of them as lines marking out what belongs to you and what is outside you. In each of the pocket books within the **Attachment Aware School Series** I have helped you to start defining your own boundaries as a member of this **Team**, outlining what your roles and responsibilities are, and what the other **Team** member's boundaries are. It's important in this particular support work that we each remain within our boundaries. It may feel at times that others might find you unreasonable or inflexible, but for the sake of yourself, the pupil in your care and the other **Team Pupil** members it is essential that you hold them.

Why do we need boundaries?
To stay healthy and well we need to know our boundaries and our limits. This is responsible, ethical practice. To not use boundaries could mean that we move out into unchartered territories that might actually cause difficulties to both the pupil and the others in **Team Pupil**, preventing recovery and maybe aggravating the situation further.

EXERCISE TO BUILD AWARENESS
THINK ABOUT THE FOLLOWING QUESTIONS:

- How do you feel about being part of **Team Pupil**?
- What experiences do you have of working in a team? List them. Note the pros and cons of working in a team.
- What do you think you will contribute personally to this team? What are your strengths, gifts and abilities?
- How will you stay connected with **Team Pupil** in the midst of a busy school term?
- How will you stay connected to your pupil once demands kick in?
- What will you do to ensure and affirm your separateness, as both are needed - separateness and togetherness?
- When things go wrong as they will from time to time, what will you do to encourage each other to persevere?
- If and when your pupil rejects you or doesn't give you back what usual relating does, how will you ensure you do not shift into blocked care? If you do, how will you flag up your needs to the rest of **Team Pupil**?
- How will you look after yourself and each other?

Team Pupil in school

How do we let others beyond Team Pupil know our boundaries?

Be kind, respectful and firm when holding your boundaries around the work of **Team Pupil** with those who are not part of the **Team**. There is no need to make a big fuss about this. Just state calmly and briefly what you will be doing, and in some cases what you won't be doing. When you state this you are in effect marking your boundary lines out again to remind the others around you. Sometimes they have overstepped the boundaries without even realising, so be gracious! They may feel awful for having gone too far without noticing what was happening. Do check out how you are feeling when you are stating your boundaries with others, and ensure you are in contact with **Team Pupil** to have others on board, to help you be clear and remain steady if there is challenge.

I have had to use boundaries a lot in my work. There are some people for whom personal and professional boundaries are really, really hard. For example, they haven't learned yet that it is OK to say No and to defend their 'territory' or specific area of work. Because of where they are on this issue, they can easily intrude upon others' boundaries; this is what is happening to them, after all! When you meet someone like this, there's a need to be gentle but strong with your assertiveness. If you don't, you could easily lose a sense of who you are and what you are about. Let them know clearly what you are doing, and why, even if you need to keep repeating yourself. I now realise that it doesn't matter whether other people do 'get it' for themselves, or not. I simply need to focus on ensuring I give the best I can, on behalf of the troubled pupils I come alongside, by holding my boundaries effectively.

How do we respect other's boundaries?

Of course the same is true for those around us. Our pupils will have their own windows of tolerance and our colleagues will be doing all they can to hold their boundaries too. In all our practice we need to be respectful. It may be that you don't agree with the other's perspective or perception, and if you don't, please may I encourage you to continue building connection? I can assure you that if you spend enough quality time with the other person you will start to understand why they do what they do and this will increase your patience levels! There will be times when we might want to gently challenge others, but we can only do this if we have earned the right through relationship. Don't ever enter into manipulation, as it will deeply damage trust. Maintain integrity throughout.

B WORKING IN PARTNERSHIP TO SETTLE THE PUPIL

Let's consider the 3 R's again, but this time on behalf of the pupil (*see* p.38). In all our interactions it will be important to first soothe the lower parts of the brain before

Team Pupil in school

getting onto anything too cognitive. We will need to consider mind-body interventions. Sadly, in our schools we sometimes think we can *think* our way out of difficulties, as in, 'if only the pupil would realise the consequences of his actions, he would change his behaviour'. However, things are not that simple when trauma is in the mix and we are relating to developmentally vulnerable brains. Instead, we need to consider respecting our pupil's nervous system and everything that's going on there on a *physical* level, and then on an *emotional* level, before we get *cognitive*, if at all, at least initially. There are some pupils who are going to need to borrow our thinking brains for some while yet as they are still functioning very much from their emotional brains. Think toddler, despite the pupil being so much older.

If you're really keen on the neuroscience of what's happening, have a look at the polyvagal theory (*outlined in* **STL**) and documented well in *Brain Based Parenting* by Dan Hughes & Jon Baylin (2012) or go deeper by considering the work of Stephen Porges, whose work Hughes & Baylin draw and build on so effectively.

So the 3 R's - Regulate, Relate and Reason ... (Perry, 2014). Our first port of call always needs to be to *regulate* the pupil. Think about where they are in their states continuum (*opposite*) and aim to shift them always into a state of calm alert by using food, drink, movement, exercise. Don't focus on words at this point!

Cognitive state	Abstract	Concrete	Emotional	Reactive	Reflexive
Internal state	Calm	Alert	Alarm	Fear	Terror

From Perry, 2003

The second stage will already be something both the Key Pupil and the Key Adult are familiar with, because they'll have been regularly engaging in regulation tasks and activities together, for example both having a hot chocolate - and this stage is, to *relate*. It's not about drinking the hot chocolate in a relational vacuum! It's making it together and enjoying it together as part of getting to know each other, making connection with each other in relationship. The power of connection is often underestimated. We are often too quick to want to get logical, spelling out the *ifs* and *if nots*, the *thens*, the cause and effect, the consequences. Instead we need to build a platform for us to then move together into *reason* at a later time. Engage in PACE (*see below*, and *see* Interventions on pp.44-5). Enter into the dance of attachment with your pupil.

Only after having attended to the first two R's can you really go into any kind of Reasoning. And when you do, keep it brief and to the point - these pupils will not take in lectures! If you need to build in reparation of any kind, do

Team Pupil in school

ensure you continue to regulate stress and shame levels: it is our responsibility to keep these both low in view of supporting pupils with fried nervous systems. There are many ways to enable these pupils to engage in reparation and discipline already discussed in **STL** and in **WAM**.

PACE (Huges 2009)

> **P** for *playfulness*. Give yourself permission to smile, to laugh and to play - whatever the age of your pupil! We do not play enough. The best way to cement a relationship is to play together. Have fun. The more shared joy experiences we can cultivate, the better.
>
> **A** for communicating *acceptance*. Show the pupil that you 'get' what they are attempting to communicate especially through their behaviour. You may not necessarily agree with the behaviour but our first step is to build a platform whereby our pupils feel 'heard'. If they don't, they are likely to shift their behaviour up another level to attempt to get your attention in a last desperate attempt to feel understood. In all my support groups for education staff I always say, "*Stay with the uncomfortable feelings for*

longer than feels comfortable," even if that's only two minutes more. Active listening is more powerful than you may ever realise.

C for developing *curiosity*. See yourself as a bit of a detective. Watch, wait and wonder (Muir & Lojkasek 1999). Notice out loud. Wonder out loud. This will feel odd to begin with, but you will become a natural after a while! We commentate frequently with babies and toddlers, but stop noticing and wondering as they get older. Why do we stop? It is such a helpful strategy. It builds value, worth and self-awareness. I have heard countless examples now of Key Adults telling me that their pupils respond to such comments with an open expression, and can sometimes even seem bewildered that you are attempting to make sense of who they are.

E is for communicating *empathy*. At any and every opportunity top them up with empathy. The more you give out, the more they receive, the more they are likely to pass on! It's a win/win!

Team Pupil in school

C RESILIENCE

i Increasing connection

Whatever we do we must honor and protect relationships, especially the stability of relationships, even if that means using scaffolding for our Key Pupils for a period of time until the relationship holds stronger. Theraplay, PACE and DDP (*see* **Useful Contacts**) can really shift old mindsets and give pupils who have been relationally wounded fresh ways of looking at themselves and the others around them. So many of these children and young people are haunted by ghosts of the past and need specialist support to help move them forward, otherwise they are at risk of becoming stuck seeing life through the lens of insecure attachment, and behaving accordingly.

This will mean not mixing and matching staff, because of the fear of dependency which is still around in some of our schools. It is about allowing pupils the opportunity to develop and deepen genuine relationship with the same Key Adult and colleagues in **Team Pupil** over two to three years at least! As I describe throughout this Series and promote through all my work, relationships are the most effective vehicles towards adaption and recovery. Your Key Pupil needs you to communicate how much you value these relationships and want to invest in them, by giving your fellow **Team** members protected time together with your shared Key Pupil, and by encouraging families to have special mother/daughter, father/son days and Lee time on a Thursday and Sîan time on a

Wednesday! They need to know that we rate relationships as important and something to be treasured and developed further. We can't just talk about all this. The pupils need rich, relational experiences, not simply words and good intentions. That is what will genuinely build their resilience.

ii Individual strengths and abilities

As discussed in the Key Teacher's pocket book (**KTiS**) it is essential that we identify what makes this particular Key Pupil tick. Each of us has something special, as Ken Robinson talks about extensively in *The Element* (2010). For some, that gift or those gifts are overshadowed or buried away because of so much pain and the masks that have been unconsciously created to defend against any further possibility of vulnerability. I don't think we always account for the fact that when we use our defences, they become generalised and don't differentiate between pain and joy. So, many of our pupils will not really allow themselves to feel the pleasure of doing well at something or of feeling the joy of being totally engaged in something, because they are so shielded and defended against the pain of not doing well, not feeling safe enough to risk making mistakes or allowing themselves to let go and concentrate and become immersed. One day, when the warmth of our connection has melted away their defences, they will be able to know what their element is. However, until that day, we are going to have to 'set them up,' so to speak, surrounding them with opportunities that can support them to thrive. And we will have to do the noticing and the making links.

Team Pupil in school

iii Being part of teams/clubs

Team Pupil can really help engage your Key Pupil in teams and clubs that are matched to their interests, whenever possible. However, I need to point out that many of the children and young people whom I work with find it very hard to walk into a group without first having a contact whom they know, someone they could meet beforehand, or meet there. It is too risky not knowing what they are walking into, so please provide stepping stones, rather than expecting them just to arrive. Many won't make it! Whenever I run any arts projects, our team always visits the pupil at home and attempts to connect him or her with someone else their age or with similar interests quite quickly.

iv Developing a tool bank of strategies

Please don't ever assume these pupils know what to do when:

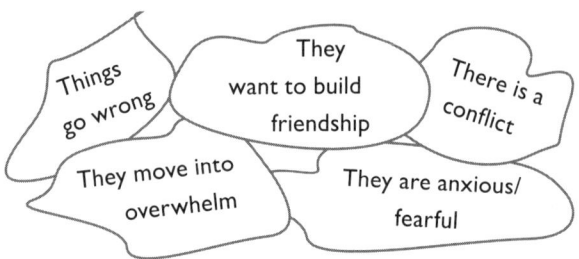

- Things go wrong
- They want to build friendship
- There is a conflict
- They move into overwhelm
- They are anxious/fearful

See it as part of your **Team's** role to support the pupil with opportunities to identify, practise and strengthen their tool bank in these key areas whenever they come up, as they will in day-to-day living and time in school. Role plays of real life scenarios that are going on in the pupil's life are especially powerful. Something that is especially effective is when the member of staff has a go at 'being the pupil', stating what they might say and do in response to the scenario. *"Can I have a go at being you and just thinking what I might do in that scenario? You be the other person"* (where relevant). Then check out your Key Pupil's impression, and see if he or she wants to have a go at trying that, in role play first in order to see what the fit feels like, and then testing it out in reality.

v   An extra note regarding laughter

It is important within Team Pupil that we are light hearted and playful together and with our pupil. Let's commit to ensuring that smiles, laughter and fun are high on the agenda of day-to-day life at school. Why? Well, the short and long term benefits of this are astounding; so why would we bypass them?

In the short term, laughter:

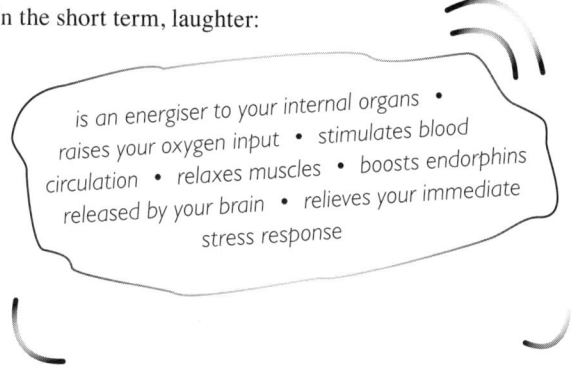

is an energiser to your internal organs • raises your oxygen input • stimulates blood circulation • relaxes muscles • boosts endorphins released by your brain • relieves your immediate stress response

Team Pupil in school

In the long term, laughter:

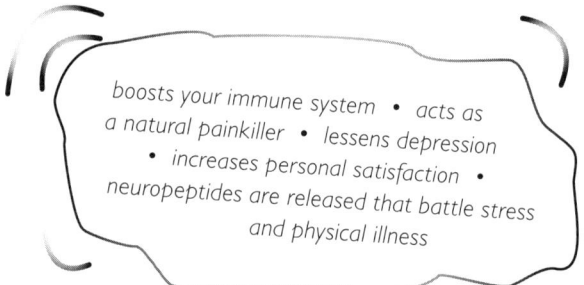

boosts your immune system • acts as a natural painkiller • lessens depression • increases personal satisfaction • neuropeptides are released that battle stress and physical illness

Meyer (2016) says laughter is like internal jogging. I love this! Let's ensure everyone gets opportunity to stay healthy by encouraging this internal jogging.

Staying inspired

I don't know how many people saw the trailer for the Paralympics in summer 2016, but I was blown away by it. Such creative energy, power and skill captured in only three minutes. If you haven't seen it already, please watch (youtube/IocLkk3aYlklink). Remember that disability isn't only about what we see but what we don't see as well. Many of our children and young people have disabilities in their mental health because of everything they have experienced. Some will recover completely. Some will need to learn to adapt and to press forwards, despite their vulnerabilities. What inspiration is contained in these three minutes … "*I can* …" Let's use what could be considered as our weakness for strength! Who knows what might be possible …

D ADVOCACY

These children will probably need our advocacy with the following people and contexts:

- Between peers
- With the class
- With a member of Team Pupil
- With their own parent/carer
- With the other parents
- With the governors
- With the wider community
- With another school/college/university
- With their social worker if they have one
- With the wider school staff

So the Key Adult will be having regular contact with parents and carers, regular email exchanges as well as face-to-face time. The Key Teacher(s) may be leading conversations with their classes about difference and diversity, ensuring that all pupils know that they can expect their needs to be given consideration and attention, and sharing what they have noticed about their Key Pupil's strengths and abilities with other colleagues in the staffroom who also teach the pupil. The Senior Manager may be involved with arranging attachment aware training for staff, consulting with external therapists to provide specialist input for **Team Pupil**, or enabling an Ofsted inspector to have more understanding of why your Key Pupil may well have a spikey profile, and how **Team Pupil** is supporting him or her where they are now.

Team Pupil in school

And any or all of you may be involved when conflict situations and disruptions arise, as can often be the case during the recovery of a child or young person who has experienced **relational trauma** and loss. So, please be prepared to step in and lend your thinking brain (pre-frontal cortex - the more mature and complex part of the brain) to represent your shared Key Pupil. Sometimes you will need to be a real pacifier, directly intervening to bring peace to an already enflamed situation. Other times, you may be able to practise tools and strategies with your Key Pupil, as I mentioned above in the last section, once you reach the Reasoning stage and can engage in reparation together.

However, more than likely you are going to need to be a translator on behalf of your Key Pupil - your wonderings about why they did, what they did and; and, with your Key Pupil, on behalf of the other person - your wonderings about why *they* did what they did. A human bridge is so often needed especially at the beginning, when your Key Pupil is still discovering and learning about security for the first time. There is a lot of risk around when you are insecure. Let's appreciate this and be so very, very patient, stay close and in contact and draw on each other whilst we do so. This collective approach is one of the great strengths of the **Team Pupil** approach.

E HOLDING ONTO SUCCESS

From working alongside children, families and schools I am all too aware of the way we can quickly move on from the successes to the difficulties which take our constant focus. But a big determinant of dreaming big is based on what has already gone on before! So **Team Pupil** needs to get much better at pressing the pause button and processing the journey you have made together thus far. You can do this in all kinds of ways, for example:

> *Thinking about the journey*
> - A case study
> - A memory book
> - A portfolio of success (snapping anything that is healthy and appropriate)
> - Befores and Afters list
> - Parts picture work (see **IIH**)
> - Commentating
> - Writing a therapeutic story for your Key Pupil about your experience of him or her (see **IIH** and Golding 2014)

Let's explore and reflect on the journey travelled so far and what it has cost, in terms of risk for your Key Pupil.

Team Pupil in school

Don't ever underestimate the cost when there is insecurity around! There are so many Big Asks, especially in the school context (*and see* p.32).

Also ensure you reflect together as a **Team** on what is getting stronger in your Key Pupil. It is too easy to focus on the journey that still lies ahead. We are in this for the long haul and so supporting each other to engage in reflective dialoguing, processing what's happened and learning from it as a **Team**, will all play a significant contribution to your own resilience.

When the going gets tough, it is helpful to have something that you can refer to that is not just a memory, but something more concrete that you can look at and touch, like the success book or even what you have written so far in your case study. We all lose our capacity to think clearly, and it's so helpful to draw on positive memories when we are alarmed. The better we get at this in our small teams, the more we will be able to stand our ground when the going gets tough or if others become cynical around us. We need to be big enough, strong enough, wise enough and kind enough to keep going! (**Circle of Security®**)

As I mentioned earlier, it is a real privilege to be able to contribute to the life of a pupil in this way, by becoming part of their special **Team**. You may well be one of the first adults that he or she experiences as present, attentive, attuned and responsive. What a privilege! And when you start seeing the impact of your support, typically after around 18 months, what a joy that will be! The investment you're all making together now will be SO worth it. I know as I have been there, journeying with very many pupils now over the years. Some big shifts can also happen between 18 months to 3 years so please do keep going! Remember you are leaving this pupil so much that is incredibly precious that will be theirs to keep as they journey on through life. You could literally be the difference between life and death in some cases. Because without genuine relational input and connection, pupils who have experienced **relational trauma** and loss are very much at risk of mental health difficulties, addictions and even self harm and suicide.

We are all designed to be interconnected, so let's pave the way for this type of healthy living for our Key Pupils. And in all our interventions, let's encourage our pupils to choose whatever is lovely, right and good for them, and for others.

Team Pupil in school

Glossary

Additional attachment figure This is the person selected in school to get alongside a child with attachment difficulties, here described as the **Key Adult**. This person could be a teaching/learning assistant or teacher, or mentor. The task is to relate to the child using strategies derived from attachment and developmental principles. Their aim is to create a relationship which will facilitate opportunities for second chance learning, so that the child can have the experience of making healthier attachments than previously. These experiences encourage the development of neural connections in the brain, which in turn leads to the development of conscience, cause-and-effect thinking, logic and empathy.

Attachment history A child's history of significant relationships and the security, or lack of security, safety, or lack of safety, of those relationships with parents, wider family, carers or adopters. It may also include other significant individuals including teachers or even pets. Any type of trauma and loss is especially important to note, even if a loss had been deemed to be in the best interest of the child (for example, loss of contact with an abusive parent): as is any kind of extraordinary stress experienced. We need to know what they have lived through from pregnancy onwards, if there has been any kind of potential disruption to the usual bonding/attachment process.

Team Pupil in school

Attachment Lead An Attachment Lead is an appointed and trained member of staff in the school who seeks to lead the way in attachment awareness and trauma informed interventions and embed them into policy on behalf of troubled pupils. This is usually a member of support staff on the ground leading through practice with individual pupils, and a member of Senior Management leading through advocacy and strategic action amongst the whole school community. See www.attachmentleadnetwork.net for more information on the training required.

Attachment system An innate urge within humans (and other mammals) that impels us to seek promixity to and relationship with others. Attachment serves two important functions: a protective function and a secure base effect. It is in our interest to stay close to another person, especially when we are very young, defenceless and vulnerable. Staying close can keep us safe. It is also in our interest to have someone to act as our **secure base**. If we have a secure base, we are then freed up to set off out of our comfort zone into the unfamiliar, the unknown, into unchartered territory - the world is ours to be curious and learn about. We can do this knowing that we can return to our secure base before venturing off again. Our secure base gives us the confidence we need in order to take the risks required in learning. Our attachment system (of neural connections and hormone release leading to attachment seeking behaviour) is activated if we experience anxiety.

Blocked care According to Hughes & Baylin (2012), when a child or adolescent continually rejects care and nurture from an adult, the brain systems that support empathy within the adult begin to close down as a protective response. The adult can feel frustrated, irritated, hopeless, rejecting or numb. They may continue to provide care, from a position of 'duty', but find it difficult or impossible to relate to the child from the loving and open engaged stance necessary for authentic and healing relationship (**STL** p.324).

Circle of Security® The Circle of Security® is a relationship based early intervention programme designed to enhance attachment security between parents and children. Decades of university-based research have confirmed that secure children exhibit increased empathy, greater self-esteem, better relationships with parents and peers, enhanced school readiness, and an increased capacity to handle emotions more effectively when compared with children who are not secure. The Circle of Security® intervention and the graphic designed around it are intended to help caregivers increase their awareness of their children's needs and whether their own responses meet those needs. With increased awareness, parents can expand their moment-to-moment parenting choices where needed. In this shift from mind-blindness to seeing what is hidden in plain sight lies the potential to break the stranglehold of problematic attachment patterns, passed from one generation to the next, that can compromise healthy relationships throughout a child's life span. (*With thanks to Jenny Peters and Glen Cooper*)

Containment When a baby is distressed or dysregulated, she needs repeated experiences of her parent or carer being 'bigger, stronger, wiser and kinder' (**Circle of Security®**) to help to 'hold' her feelings and experience and make sense of what is happening, until she is able to do this for herself. Similarly, adult individuals and teams need **Senior Managers** who can create containing environments to support their work containing children who have experienced **relational trauma**.

Developmental Trauma A term used by Van der Kolk (2014) and many other attachment aware and trauma informed practitioners to describe a child's experiences of repeated or prolonged trauma through neglect, abuse, abandonment, violence, loss, parental substance misuse or addiction. Developmental trauma implies that the child's developing brain will have been impacted, with negative effects on the development of their executive functions,

Team Pupil in school

motor skills, and capacity to self-regulate, communicate and relate. Left unattended at home and/or in school, the effects of developmental trauma are likely to persist into adulthood and have profound effects on every aspect of the individual's life.

Disrupted relationships/connections Relationships and connections that have been disrupted or compromised for the individual child through having early experiences of loss, abuse, neglect, trauma, domestic violence, or parental substance abuse or mental ill health. Disruption isn't necessarily intentional (although it can be) but can come about due to circumstance: for example, medical complications at birth, having a mother who becomes unwell after birth … the ordinary development of brain connections may have been disrupted if these experiences happen at certain crucial times, or for prolonged periods. Disruptions often compromise or disrupt trust. There are many children in our care who have experienced intimacy betrayals at the hands of their own birth parents. The deep distrust that has been created out of relational experience is then often projected onto other adults, regardless of their intentions or motives. We can in fact get caught up in their time-warp, experiencing the distress, grief and rage intended for someone else, in another time and place.

Exploratory system An innate urge within humans (and other mammals) that impels us to explore, experiment, play, and thereby learn. The exploratory system (of neural connections and hormone release leading to exploratory behaviour) is activated or reaches its full potential when the attachment system is well attended to. If the attachment system is not attended to, the exploratory system (which is needed for learning) will be impeded by ongoing anxiety.

Hypervigilance A subliminal rapid-reaction mammalian defence developed in response to repeated or continual traumatic experience. The individual becomes wired for a state of high alert at all times to any potential danger in the environment, thus 'primed for threat'. He or she may view or interpret events, words or actions as dangerous which others around them view as innocent or innocuous.

Insecure attachment This indicates a level of insecurity that interferes with the child's ability to relate in a healthy or appropriate way to other people. Such insecurity arose from early uncertainties about the reliability of his or her parent or primary carer. We can observe too much dependence or too much independence in his response to his needs and the satisfaction of those needs. There are traditionally three main types of insecure attachment, sometimes described as avoidant, ambivalent and disorganised.

Primary Attachment Figure This is the person who takes the main caring/parenting role for the child at home. It could be a parent, grandparent, foster carer, adoptive parent, kinship carer or residential children's worker. The person is someone on whom the child is dependent for many needs including safety, and for being able to develop in all ways, including the ability to make and maintain relationships. The experience that a child has with his primary attachment figure will shape his view of himself, others and the world around him.

Regulatory system If we have received consistent and sufficient regulatory experiences ourselves, through being attuned to and received by calming and soothing others, especially in our early years, then we are more able to internalise what becomes our own regulatory system (internal and external tools and strategies) to help us self-regulate at times of stress. If, however, we haven't had appropriate calming and soothing, at the right time, then our regulatory systems can be over-active and we can end up becoming dysregulated very frequently, even for everyday ordinary stressors. This is why many of our pupils need so much help with regulation.

Team Pupil in school

Relational buffering Rich relational connection serves a protective function. It provides protection from the full impact of stress. It prevents stress from becoming toxic and damaging us. Those who have experienced relational poverty/withdrawal or trauma are very vulnerable and fragile in the midst of everyday ordinary stressors, as well as extraordinary **toxic stress**. This puts them at further risk.

Many of the pupils in our care who have experienced significant **relational trauma** and loss had to manage big overwhelming states, sensations and feelings on their own. Because this occurred when their developing nervous systems were very fragile, they have learned to rely on their feeling brain, and primitive limbic system in relation to stressors that come their way.

If we can now stand in the gap and give these pupils the sensitive, attuned care that they didn't have or didn't have enough of in their early years, then we are in effect providing them with the relational buffering they need in order to interrupt the impulsivity that occurs by using the emotional brain in isolation. We can in effect become like 'external brains', lending them our thinking brain to inhibit impulsivity, until they can manage for themselves. Check out the 'handbrain model' on Youtube, by Daniel Siegel.

Relational trauma Trauma experienced by the child on a repeated basis within the context of relationship (often from within early attachments) eg abuse, neglect, violence, intrusion, loss, abandonment and so on. The child may well have experienced overwhelm, powerlessness and terror in the process. The child may well now be completely confused as to the role and purpose of adults, having experienced such overwhelm in their care. It is not surprising therefore that coming into contact with us is going to mean them moving into pseudo-independent states, however caring we may try to be.

Relative dependency This term describes what we may be able to facilitate in schools, in order to give a child who has experienced early **relational trauma** and loss an opportunity for learning, trust and security through the relationship with a consistent adult who offers sensitive care: in this case, the **Key Adult**.

Safe space A protected area/space or room full of sensory comfort to support a pupil either to upregulate or downregulate dependent on their state. This space is not used as an area for relational withdrawal or isolation but of time with the Key Adult. There is no expectation there will be talking; the best use of the area is to 'be together'. However both adult and pupil may engage in sensory activites, Theraplay® and PACE. The Key Adult learns the pupil and knows what is needed.

Secondary stress When an individual has experienced profound trauma, those working and living with them are likely to experience stress within their relationships and contact. This stress is a physiological and psychological reality, and those affected will need to seek their own support to help manage it.

Secure attachment This indicates a healthy and appropriate style of relating to other people. An interplay of dependence and independence is observed in response to needs and the satisfaction of those needs, as well as empathy for and generosity towards others.

Secure base A term used by Sir John Bowlby to describe what a 'significant other' (eg. a parent/carer at home, or a Key Adult in school) can become if he or she provides 'good enough' care for a child. It is from this base that a child can become free to explore and engage with the learning process in school. Equally a room with supportive colleagues can provide a 'secure base' for staff (see **attachment system**).

Team Pupil in school

Social Engagement System Described by Stephen Porges (*please see* (**STL**) p.80) as the open and engaged state achieved when an individual feels safe, and from which the individual will invite communication, understanding and joint interest in the immediate situation with another person.

Splitting When a child presents with a pattern of disorganised and insecure attachment, the adults around him or her may, in response to the strong feelings stirred up by the child's behaviour and responses, become polarised in their view of him or her and each other. Blame and division can easily develop. **Team Pupil** and the wider system around the child need to find support so that this 'splitting' can be resolved in the interests of the child and of preserving best working practices and relationships.

Toxic stress We all experience ordinary stressors in life. However if a child with a fragile and developing nervous system experiences extraordinary stressors, for example at the hands of his or her own parents, over a period of time, then the child can move into overwhelm. This overwhelm, which can include being flooded with high levels of stress hormones for significant periods, can put undue pressure on the developing body and brain, heart and mind, meaning that their natural development and functioning may become disrupted. This may lead to the state described as 'developmental vulnerability', or trauma.

References

Aspden, K.L. (2015) *Help! I've got an alarm bell going off in my head! How panic, anxiety and stress affect your body* London: Jessica Kingsley Publishers

Belsky, J., Vandell, D.L., Burchinal, M., Clarke-Stewart, K.A., McCartney, K., Owen, M.P. & The NICHD Early Child Care Research Network (2007) Are There Long-Term Effects of Early Child Care? *Child Development* Vol 78, (2)pp.681-701

Bombèr, L.M. (2007) *Inside I'm Hurting: Practical strategies for supporting children with attachment difficulties in schools* London: Worth Publishing

Bombèr, L.M. (2009) Survival of the fittest: teenagers finding their way through the labyrinth of transitions in schools *in*, Perry, A. (Ed.) *Teenagers and Attachment: Helping adolescents engage with life and learning*
London: Worth Publishing

Bombèr, L.M. (2011) *What About Me? Inclusive strategies to support pupils with attachment difficulties make it through the school day* London: Worth Publishing

Bombèr, L.M. & Hughes, D. (2013) *Settling to Learn: Why relationships matter in schools* London: Worth Publishing

Bombèr, L.M. (2015) *The Key Adult in School, Attachment Aware Schools Series Book 1* Duffield, Derbyshire: Worth Publishing

Bombèr, L.M. (2016) *The Senior Manager in School, Attachment Aware Schools Series Book 2* Duffield, Derbyshire: Worth Publishing

Bombèr, L.M. (2016) *The Key Teacher in School, Attachment Aware Schools Series Book 3* Duffield, Derbyshire: Worth Publishing

Team Pupil in school

Booth, P. & Jernberg, A. (2010) *Theraplay: Helping parents and children build better relationships through attachment based play* New York: John Wiley & Sons

Brown, B. (2012) *Daring Greatly: How the courage to be vulnerable transforms the way we live, love, parent and lead* London: Penguin Books Ltd

Brown, B. (2010) *Ted Talk on Vulnerability* ted.com/talks/brene_brown_on_vulnerability?language=en

Cameron, C., Connelly, G. & Jackson, S. (2015) *Educating Children and Young People in Care* London: Jessica Kingsley

Circle of Security youtube clip youtube.com/watch?v=F6DhnbgRAOo Shark Music vimeo.com/145329119

Clarke, J. & Dawson, C. (1998) *Growing Up Again* Minnesota, USA: Hazelden

Cozolino, L. (2013) *The Social Neuroscience of Education:Optimizing attachment and learning in the classroom* New York: WW Norton

Cozolino, L. (2014) *The Neuroscience of Human Relationships: A practical guide for the inner journey* New York: WW Norton

Forbes, H. (2011) *Overwhelm - Beyond Consequences: Parenting Solutions* Youtube v=X9zLKSoYOaO

Forbes, H. (2012) *Help for Billy: A Beyond Consequences approach to helping challenging children in the classroom* Beyond Consequences Institute, LLC. beyondconsequences.com

Geddes, H. (2006) *Attachment in the Classroom* London: Worth Publishing

Golding, K. S. (2007) *Nurturing Attachments. Supporting children who are fostered or adopted.* London, Jessica Kingsley

Golding, K., Fain, J., Frost, A., Mills, C., Worrall, H., Roberts, N., Durant, E. & Templeton, S. (2012) *Observing Children with Attachment Difficulties in School: A tool for identifying and supporting emotional and social difficulties in children* London: Jessica Kingsley

Golding, K. & Hughes, D. (2012) *Creating Loving Attachments* London: Jessica Kingsley

Golding, K. S. (2013) *Nurturing Attachments Training Resource. Running parenting groups for adoptive parents and foster or kinship carers.* London, Jessica Kingsley

Golding, K. S. (2014) *Using Stories to Build Bridges with Traumatised Children* London: Jessica Kingsley

Greenhalgh, P. (1994) *Emotional Growth & Learning* London: Routledge

Gregory, A. & Weinstein, R.S. (2004) Connection and Regulation at Home and in School: Predicting growth in achievement for adolescents *Journal of Adolescent Research* July, Vol 19 (4) pp.405-427

Handford, M. (2104) *Where's Wally?* books UK: Walker Books

Hughes, D. (2004) *Facilitating Developmental Attachment: The road to emotional recovery and behavioural change in foster and adopted children* Maryland, USA: Aronson Inc

Hughes, D. (2009) *Principles of Attachment-Focused Parenting: Effective strategies to care for children* London: WW Norton

Hughes, D. (2013) *8 Keys to Building your Best Relationships* New York: WW Norton

Hughes, D. & Baylin, J. (2012) *Brain-Based Parenting: The neuroscience of caregiving for healthy attachment* New York: WW Norton

Hughes, D. (2016) Attachment Conference London: Centre for Child Mental Health, (April)

Johnstone, M. (2012) *Quiet the Mind* London: Robinson

Karst, P. (2000) *The Invisible String* Camarilla, CA: Devorss & Co

Kintsugi youtube.com/watch?v=EBUTQkaSSTY
youtube.com/watch?v=IT55_u8URU0

Magorian, M. (2014) *Goodnight Mr Tom* London: Puffin Classic

Maté, G. (2013) *Attachment and Brain Development* YouTube/v=UbiWLLYSZhc

Mayo Clinic mayoclinic.org/healthy-lifestyle/stress-management/in-depth/stress-relief/art-20044456?pg=1

Team Pupil in school

Meyer. J (2016) *Overload: How to unplug, unwind and free yourself from the pressure of stress* London: Hodder & Stoughton

Music, G. (2011) *Nurturing Natures: Attachment and children's emotional, sociocultural and brain development* Hove: Psychology Press

Music, G. (2014) *The Good Life: Wellbeing and the new science of altruism, selfishness and immorality* Hove, UK: Routledge

Olson, K. (2014) *The Invisible Classroom: Relationships, neuroscience & mindfulness in school* New York: WW Norton

Palmer, S. (2007) *Toxic Childhood* London: Orion

Perry, B. (1999) *Memories of Fear: How the brain stores and retrieves physiologic states, feelings, behaviours and thoughts from traumatic events* Academy version, The Child Trauma Academy Houston, Texas
childtrauma.org/wp-content/uploads/2014/12/Memories_of_Fear_Perry.pdf

Perry, B. (2010) *Born for Love: Why empathy is essential and endangered* New York: Harper Collins Publishers

Perry, B. (2014) *Brain Development and Learning* Columbus Metropolitan Club, Youtube/DXdBFFph2QQ

Powell, B., Cooper, G., Hoffman, K. & Marvin, R. (2013) *The Circle of Security Intervention: Enhancing attachment in early parent-child relationships* New York: Guildford Press

Riley, P. (2011) *Attachment Theory and the Teacher-Student Relationship: A practical guide for teachers, teacher educators and school leaders* Oxon: Routledge

Robinson, K. (2010) *The Element: How finding your passion changes everything* UK: Penguin

Siegel, D. (1999) *The Developing Mind* New York: The Guildford Press

Siegel, D. (2012) The Hand Model of the Brain
youtube.com/watch?v=gm9ClJ74Oxw

Siegel, D. & Bryson, T.P. (2012) *The Whole Brain Child: 12 proven strategies to nurture your child's developing mind* London: Robinson

Siegel, D. & Bryson, T.P. (2014) *No-Drama Discipline: The whole brain way to calm the chaos and nurture your child's developing mind* Australia & UK: Scribe

Siegel, D.J. & Bryson, T.P. (2015) *Connect and Redirect Refrigerator Sheet*
drdansiegel.com/pdf/Refrigerator%20Sheet--NDD.pdf

Street, K. (2014) *School as a Secure Base: How peaceful teachers can create peaceful schools* London: Worth Publishing

Sunderland, M. (2006) *The Science of Parenting: Practical guidance on sleep, crying, play and building emotional wellbeing for life* London: Dorling Kindersley

Sunderland, M. (2015) *Conversations that Matter: Talking with children and teenagers in ways that help* Derbyshire, UK: Worth Publishing

Sunderland, M. (2016) *Best Relationship with your Child* DVD Series
childmentalhealthcentre.org/buy-dvds/category

Taransaud, D. (2011) *You Think I'm Evil: Practical strategies for working with aggressive and rebellious adolescents* London: Worth Publishing

Thierry, B. (2015) *Teaching the Child on the Trauma Continuum* Surrey: Grosvenor House Publishing Ltd

Van der Kolk, B. (2014) *The Body Keeps the Score: Brain, mind and body in the healing of trauma* New York, US: Viking

Wetz, J. (2009) *Urban Village Schools: Putting relationships at the heart of secondary school organisation and design* UK: Calouste Gulbenkian Foundation

Wilson, D. & Newton, C. (2006) *Circle of Adults: A team approach to problem solving around challenging behaviour and emotional needs* Nottingham: Inclusive solutions

WiseUp! adoptionsupport.org/store/w-i-s-e-up-powerbook-for-children-in-foster-care

Team Pupil in school

Useful documents

Accredited Training in Children's Emotional Development and Attachment - An entitlement for all who work in our schools **Consortium for Emotional Well Being In Schools** 2013 southoverpartnership.com/wp-content/uploads/2015/04/EX_Final_Report_for_CEWBS.pdf

Carter, A. (2015) *The Carter Review of initial teacher training* (ITT) Department for Education DFE-00036-2015

Children's Attachment: Attachment in children and young people who are adopted from care, in care or at high risk of going into care **NICE guideline** Published 25 November 2015 nice.org.uk/guidance/ng26

Framework of Core Content for Initial Teacher Training (ITT) July 2016 **Department for Education**

Future in Mind: Promoting, protecting and improving our children and young people's mental health and wellbeing Dept of Health and NHS England 2015 **NHS England Publication** Gateway Reference No.02939 gov.uk/dh

Promoting the Health and Well-being of Looked After Children: Statutory guidance for local authorities, clinical commissioning groups and NHS England **Dept of Education and Dept of Health** March 2015, DFE-00105-2015

Useful contacts

Attachment Lead Network	attachmentleadnetwork.net
B.A.S.E.® Babywatching UK	base-babywatching-uk.org
Beyond Consequences	beyondconsequences.com
Bruce D. Perry, Psychiatrist	childtrauma.org
Caspari Foundation	caspari.org.uk
Centre for Child Mental Health	childmentalhealthcentre.org
The Centre for Emotional Development	emotionaldevelopment.co.uk
Child Trauma Academy	childtrauma.org
Circle of Security	circleofsecurity.net
Consortium for Emotional Well Being in Schools	jameswetz3@gmail.com
Daniel A. Hughes, Child Psychologist	danielhughes.org

Team Pupil in school

Dan Siegel, Professor of Psychiatry	drdansiegel.com
Dyadic Development Psychotherapy UK	ddpnetwork.org/uk
Heart Math	heartmath.com
Inclusive Solutions	inclusive-solutions.com
Institute for Arts in Therapy and Education London	artspsychotherapy.org
Institute for Recovery from Childhood Trauma	irct.org.uk
Nurture Group Network	nurturegroups.org
Pets as Therapy	petsastherapy.org
Theraplay®	theraplay.org
Transforming Lives for Good	tlg.org.uk